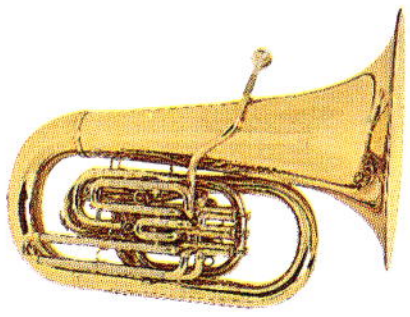

THE NEW GROLIER CHILDREN'S ENCYCLOPEDIA

2

Black hole – Conservation

GROLIER
EDUCATIONAL

Published 1999 by Grolier Educational, Danbury, CT 06816
This edition published exclusively for the school and library market

Planned and produced by Kingfisher Publications Plc,
New Penderel House, 283-288 High Holborn, London WC1V 7HZ

Set ISBN 0-7172-9373-4
Volume 2 ISBN 0-7172-9375-0

The new Grolier children's encyclopedia.
p. cm.
Rev. ed. of: The Grolier children's encyclopedia, 1994.
Summary: A ten-volume encyclopedia presenting illustrated articles, alphabetically arranged, on a wide variety of topics.
ISBN 0-7172-9373-4 (set : alk. paper). -- ISBN 0-7172-9374-2 (v. 1: alk. paper). -- ISBN 0-7172-9375-0 (v. 2: alk. paper). -- ISBN 0-7172-9376-9 (v. 3 : alk. paper)
1. Children's encyclopedias and dictionaries. [1. Encyclopedias and dictionaries.] I. Grolier Educational (Firm) II. Grolier children's encylopedia.
AG5.N34 1998
031--dc21 98-7378
CIP AC

Printed in France

INTRODUCTION

The word *encyclopedia* comes from the Greek for "all-round education," and *The Kingfisher Children's Encyclopedia* provides just that, in a way that is both accessible and stimulating.

This all-new encyclopedia covers everything from ancient history to up-to-the-minute developments in technology; from animal and plant life on Earth to plans for the next millennium in outer space. Geography, natural history, religion, the human body—all the topics that children explore at home and at school are included here.

We have rejected the "sound-bite" approach to children's reference in favor of more in-depth coverage, which makes this encyclopedia perfect for project work and homework assignments. At the same time, the text is broken up into manageable paragraphs, suitable for both confident readers and younger browsers. Colorful photographs and superb illustrations and maps not only enhance the text, but also encourage readers to find out more for themselves.

Easy access is the key to this encyclopedia. Major subject areas such as ELECTRICITY have been arranged alphabetically, but the encyclopedia also has a comprehensive index so readers can refer quickly to related topics, such as CIRCUITS and SWITCHES.

The encyclopedia has been written and checked by a team of specialist authors and consultants, and produced by a team of editors and designers with years of experience in children's reference. We are confident that it is a work in which children, and parents, can put their trust.

The Editors

Editorial Director
Jennifer Justice

U.S. Consultant
Bill Shapiro

U.S. Editor
Aimee Johnson

Managing Editor
Sarah Allen

Editorial team
Trevor Anderson, Max Benato, Jane Birch, Harry Boteler, Anne Davies, Rebecca Fry, Tracey Kelly, Sarah Kovandzich, Elizabeth Longley, Miren Lopategui, Rupert Matthews, Jayne Miller, Susan Scharpf, Brian Williams

Creative Director
Val Pidgeon

Art Director
Mike Davis

Art Editor
David Noon

Design team
Liz Black, Pete Byrne, John Jamieson, Ruth Levy, Emma Skidmore, Nina Tara

DTP Operator
Primrose Burton

Picture Research
Veneta Bullen, Davina Bullen, Sophie Mortimer, Yannick Yago

Maps
Hardlines

Contributors & Consultants
Sue Aldridge, Sarah Angliss, Max Benato, Martyn Bramwell, Enid Broderick, Tim Brown, David Burnie, Catherine Halcrow, Jack Challoner, Michael Chinery, Maria Constantino, Chris Cooper, Sophie Cooper, Alan Cowsill, Jeff Daniel, David Darling, Dougal Dixon, John Farndon, Sue Gordon, John Graham, Ian Graham, Catherine Headlam, Lesley Hill, Caroline Juler, Anne Kay, Robin Kerrod, J.C. Levy, Keith Lye, Tim Madge, David Marshall, Bob McCabe, Iain Nicolson, Steve Parker, Jane Parker, John Paton, Malcolm Porter, Sue Reid, Meg Sanders, Philip Steele, Richard Tames, John Tipler, Ian Westwell, Brian Williams

BLACK HOLE

A black hole is a region of space where the pull of gravity is so strong that nothing can escape from it, not even light.

INVISIBLE FORCE

When a black hole lies close to another star, its immense gravity sucks particles or gas away from the star. These are pulled into a gassy spiral, called an accretion disk. The gas inside the disk is heated to millions of degrees Celsius and gives off X rays. It is these powerful, flickering X rays that reveal the presence of a black hole.

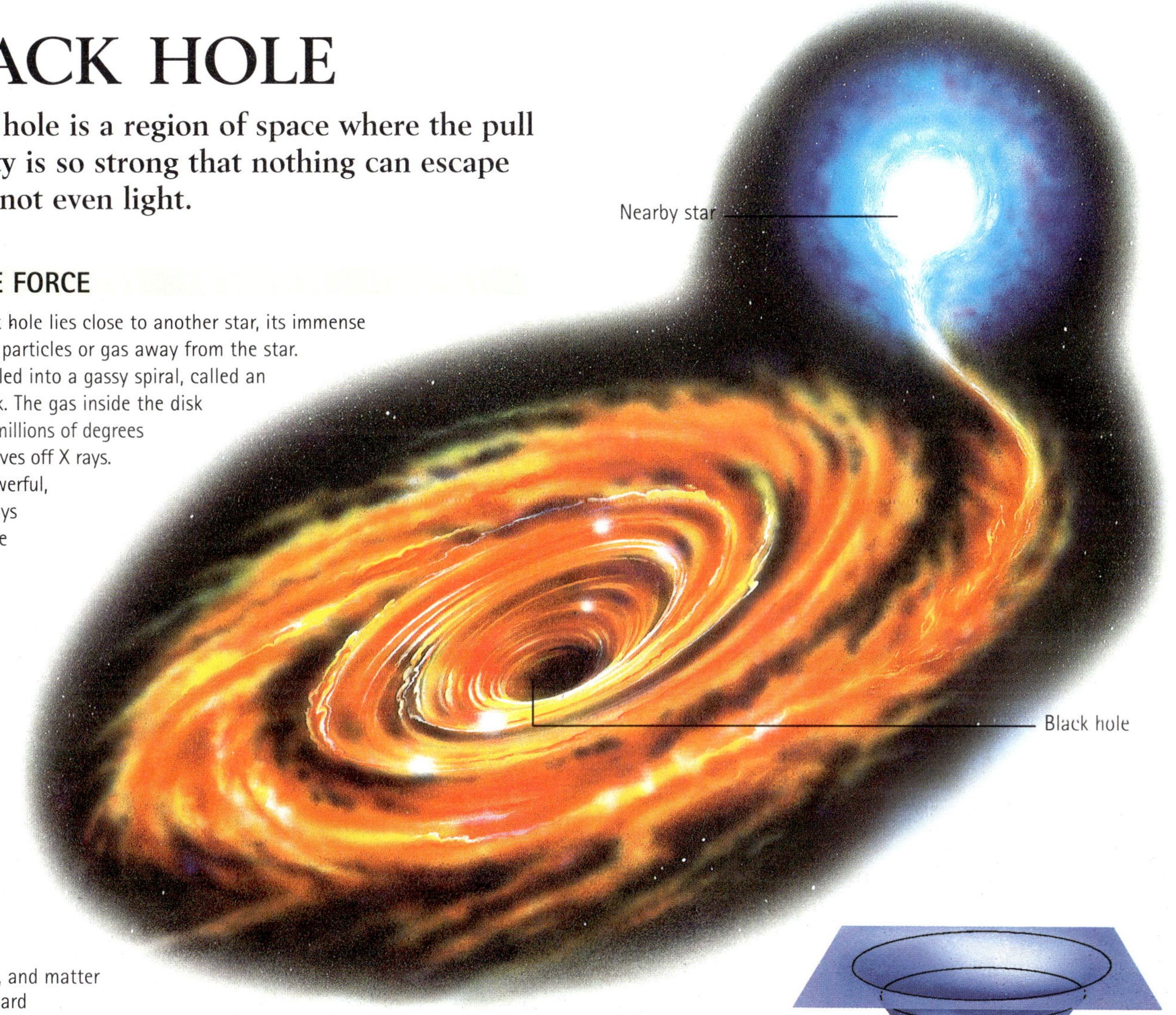

Scientists believe that a black hole forms after a massive, heavy star has exploded at the end of its life. The outer parts are hurled into space, but the core of the dead star, with no light and heat left to support it, shrinks very quickly.

DEAD STARS

The gravity of a dead star is thought to pull all the material left behind inward, squeezing it tighter to make it smaller and extremely compact. A tiny black hole, the size of a period, could hold enough matter to make a mountain. Vast black holes, thought to exist at the center of galaxies, may contain as much matter as tens of millions of stars.

COSMIC VACUUM

Black holes are invisible—they can only be tracked down by their effect on a nearby object. They tug matter away from the surface of a star, like a vacuum cleaner. This debris enters a whirlpool, which spins around the black hole before disappearing inside, like water going down a giant drain.

THROUGH A WORMHOLE

Some black holes may be the entrances to strange tunnels through space and time known as wormholes. It has been suggested that a spacecraft could travel along a wormhole and reappear in a different part of the universe.

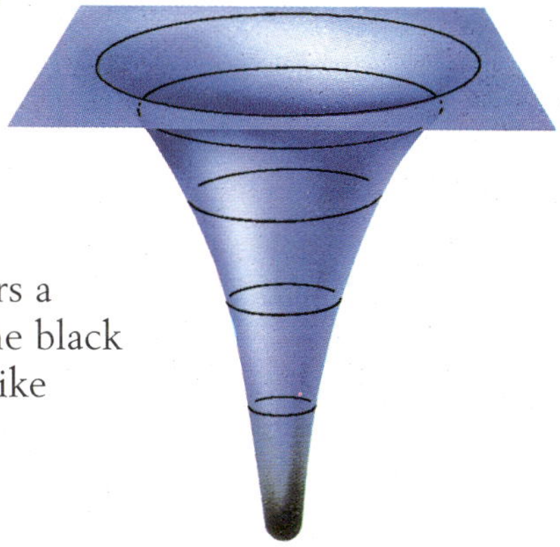

▲ A black hole is shaped like a funnel. Objects are pulled into the funnel and, once inside, never escape.

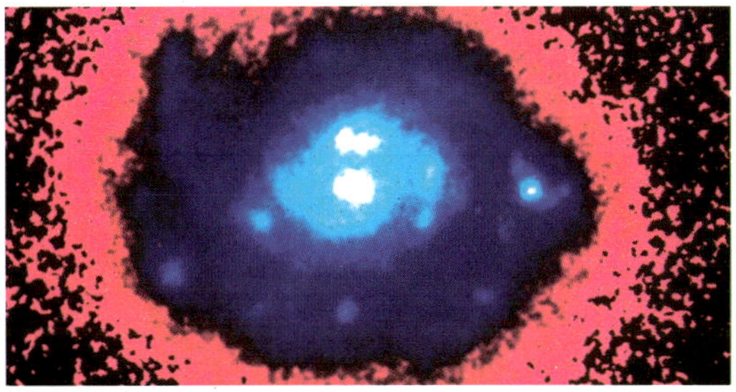

◀ This ultraviolet image shows galaxy M77. Its center is thought to be a black hole with the mass of several million suns.

SEE ALSO

Astronomy, Big Bang theory, Constellation, Galaxy, Gravity, Star

BLOOD

Blood is a vital liquid that is pumped through arteries and veins around the body by the heart. Blood carries oxygen, nutrients, hormones, and waste products.

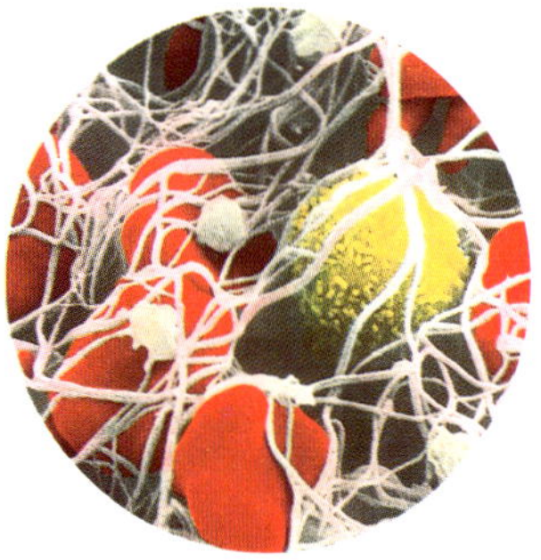

◀ Chemicals in the blood form a net over a wound. The net traps red blood cells, platelets, and white blood cells (shown in yellow) to form a clot.

KARL LANDSTEINER
This Austrian-born pathologist (1868–1943) discovered blood groups, making blood transfusions safe for the first time.

Most animals have a bloodlike fluid. It is red in most vertebrates (animals with backbones), but can be different colors in other animals. Lobsters have blue blood, snails have gray blood, some insects have green blood, and a worm's blood is colorless.

BLOOD PLASMA

Just over half (55 percent) of human blood is a pale yellow liquid called plasma. This contains hundreds of substances, including nutrients, sugars, salts, minerals, hormones, and chemicals.

OXYGEN CARRIERS

About 45 percent of blood is made up of blood cells and platelets. The vast majority of blood cells are small, red, and doughnut-shaped. They are made inside the bones and released into the blood, where they carry oxygen around the body. When red cells have plenty of oxygen, as in most arteries, they are bright red. When low in oxygen, as in most veins, they are dark red.

FAST FACTS

- An average human has 11 pt. (5l) of blood
- A blood spot the size of a pinhead contains about 5 million red cells, 10,000 white cells, and 250,000 platelets
- Anemia is a lack of oxygen in the blood

DEFENDING THE BODY

Less than one percent of blood is made up of white blood cells and platelets. There are several types of white blood cell, all of which defend the body. Some fight invading bacteria and viruses by bombarding them with chemicals. Others surround invaders and eat them.

CLOTTING AND HEALING

Platelets are cell fragments that help wounds to heal. They gather around a cut and release chemicals to slow blood loss and form a clot. This stops the blood flow and seals the wound, stopping germs from getting in while new skin grows.

BLOOD GROUPS

There are several different types of human blood, including A, B, AB, and O. The blood group depends on the chemicals that the white blood cells produce. If a person needs a blood transfusion, the right group must be given because some chemicals do not mix. The wrong chemicals may clot with the existing blood and make the illness worse or even cause death.

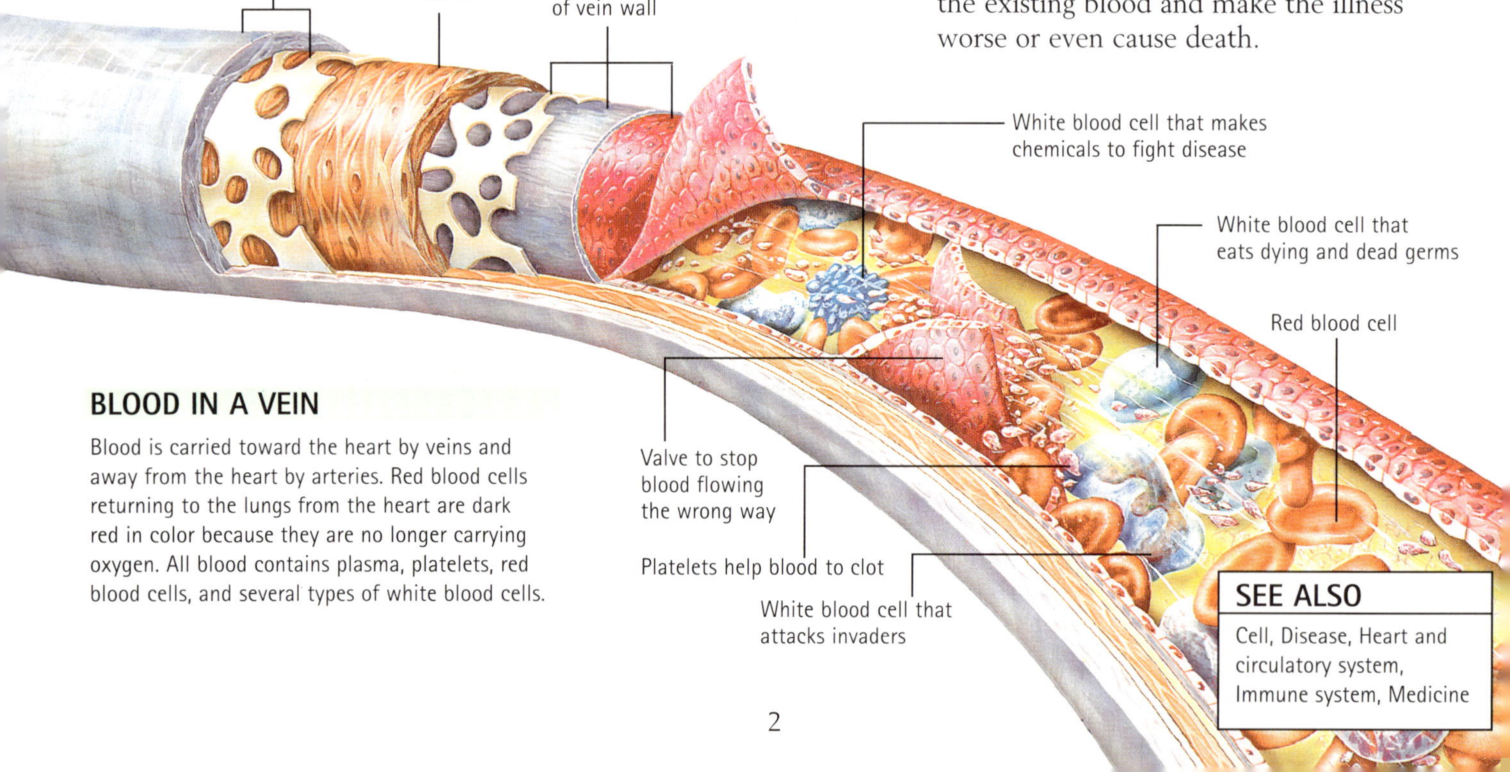

BLOOD IN A VEIN

Blood is carried toward the heart by veins and away from the heart by arteries. Red blood cells returning to the lungs from the heart are dark red in color because they are no longer carrying oxygen. All blood contains plasma, platelets, red blood cells, and several types of white blood cells.

SEE ALSO
Cell, Disease, Heart and circulatory system, Immune system, Medicine

BOAT

Boats are small watercraft powered by oars, sails, or an engine. They are smaller than ships—usually no more than about 65 ft. (20m) long.

Boats in Ancient Egypt were made by tying reed bundles together.

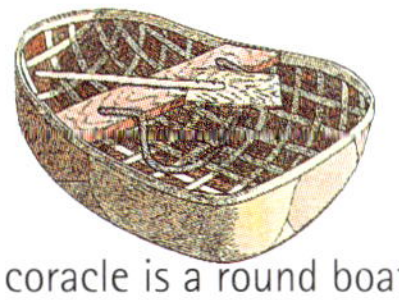

A coracle is a round boat made of animal skin stretched over a frame.

A junk is a traditional Chinese boat and is still in use today.

A catamaran is a sailboat with two hulls arranged side by side.

A paddle wheeler's engine turns a huge paddle wheel to drive the boat forward.

Small, powerful tugboats are used to tow much larger vessels into port.

POWERED BY THE WIND

The skill in sailing lies in positioning the sail so that it catches the wind most efficiently. Sails are adjusted by a sheet (rope). Sideways movement is reduced by the centerboard (keel) reaching far down into the water. The boat is steered using the tiller to adjust the position of the rudder (a board attached to the back of the boat).

► A sailboat can travel in almost any direction, but at different rates. Sailing with the wind behind the boat (running) is not the fastest. Sailing across the wind (reaching) is faster. To sail into the wind a boat must tack, or zigzag, at an angle of 45° to the wind direction with the sails drawn in as close as possible.

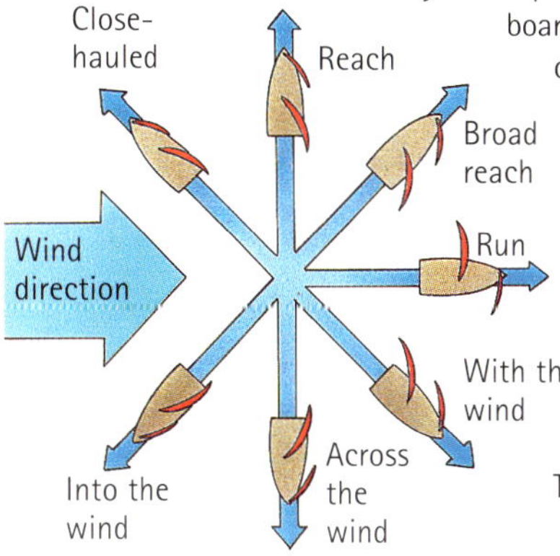

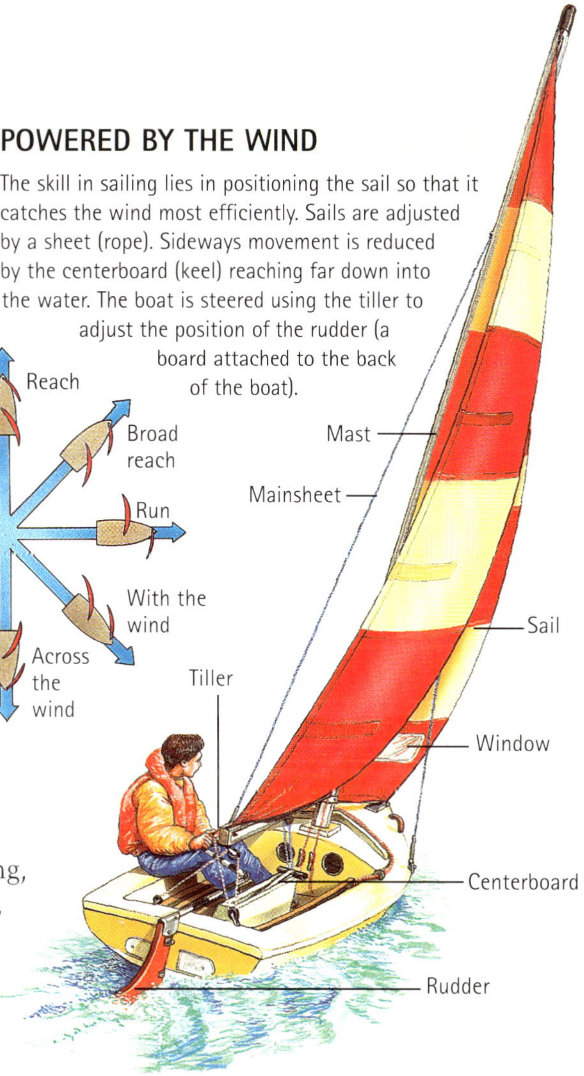

Working boats are used for fishing, transporting goods and people, and moving ships in harbors. Yachts, motorboats, sailboats, and canoes are all used for racing and for fun.

HOLLOWED-OUT TRUNKS

The first boats were built in prehistoric times, when people hollowed out tree trunks to make dugouts. Boats such as Inuit kayaks were made from animal skins, and the Ancient Egyptians made their boats from bundles of reed.

DESIGNED FOR THE JOB

A boat's design depends on its use. A lifeboat must be built to travel long distances quickly and to cope with rough seas. A small motorboat must be tough enough to withstand the pounding of the waves as well as its own engine vibrations.

PARTS OF A BOAT

The keel runs along the base of a boat. It keeps it stable and provides a framework from which to build up the boat. The hull, or outer shell, can be made of wood, but plastic and fiberglass are tougher and cheaper. The bow, or front of the boat, cuts through the water and pushes it to the sides so that the hull can glide smoothly.

ON THE MOVE

Rowboats are moved by muscle power, using oars which have a wide blade at one end. The paddles of some canoes have blades at each end and this makes it much easier to steer in fast-moving rapids. Sailboats, or yachts, use sails to catch the wind and drive them through the water. Most working boats and some sports boats are powered by an engine. This makes a propeller spin in the water, moving the boat forward.

▲ Small, light motorboats rise out of the water when they travel at speed.

SEE ALSO

Egypt, Engine, Fishing industry, Ship, Transportation, Wind power

BRAIN AND NERVOUS SYSTEM

The brain is the body's control center, responsible for action, thought, memory, behavior, and emotion. It is linked to the body by the nervous system.

Fish have simple brains, with areas that process smell extending forward to the tip of the nose.

Snakes have brains with large sight areas, showing the importance of sight for hunting.

Birds have brains with large movement centers which control the complex movements used in flight.

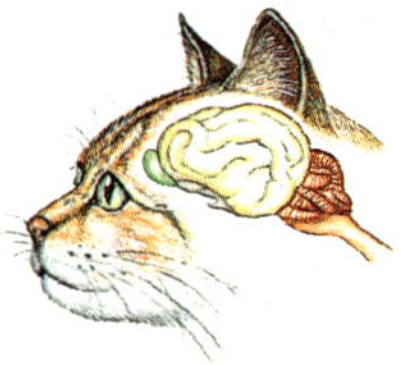

Cats, like other mammals, have brains with large cerebrums for complex and adaptable behavior.

The average adult human brain weighs about 3.1 lb. (1.4kg). It is a large grayish-colored organ. The brain is made up of tiny cells that send electrical messages to the body along a network of nerves known as the nervous system.

IN THREE PARTS

All vertebrates (animals with backbones) have a brain that can be divided into three main areas: brain stem, cerebellum, and cerebrum. The brain stem and cerebellum keep the body functioning. The cerebrum deals with thought, memory, and sensation.

THE BRAIN STEM

The brain stem is at the bottom of the brain, where it joins the spinal cord (the bundle of nerves linking the brain to the body). The stem controls the body's automatic processes, such as heartbeat, breathing, body temperature, blood pressure, digestion, and getting rid of waste.

THE CEREBELLUM

The cerebellum lies at the back of the brain. When movement instructions come from the cerebrum, the cerebellum analyzes the instructions. It then sends signals to the muscles to make smooth and coordinated movements. The cerebellum also controls posture and balance.

THE CEREBRUM

About 90 percent of the human brain is taken up by the cerebrum—the center of all thought. It is split into two halves, called cerebral hemispheres, which contain gray matter and white matter. Gray matter lies on the surface and is made up of nerve cell bodies, which create messages. The inner white matter is packed with nerve fibers carrying the messages to the body.

CEREBRAL CENTERS

The human cerebrum looks the same all over, but different areas carry out special functions. One area receives and processes nerve signals from the eyes. Another is for touch, processing nerve signals from the skin. Just in front of this is the motor

HOW NERVE CELLS PASS ON MESSAGES

The brain and nervous system are made of microscopic nerve cells called neurons. Each nerve cell has two parts: a spiderlike cell body and a long nerve fiber. The cell body receives signals from other nerve cells and passes these along its fiber, like a tiny telephone wire, to yet more nerve cells, until the message reaches its final destination.

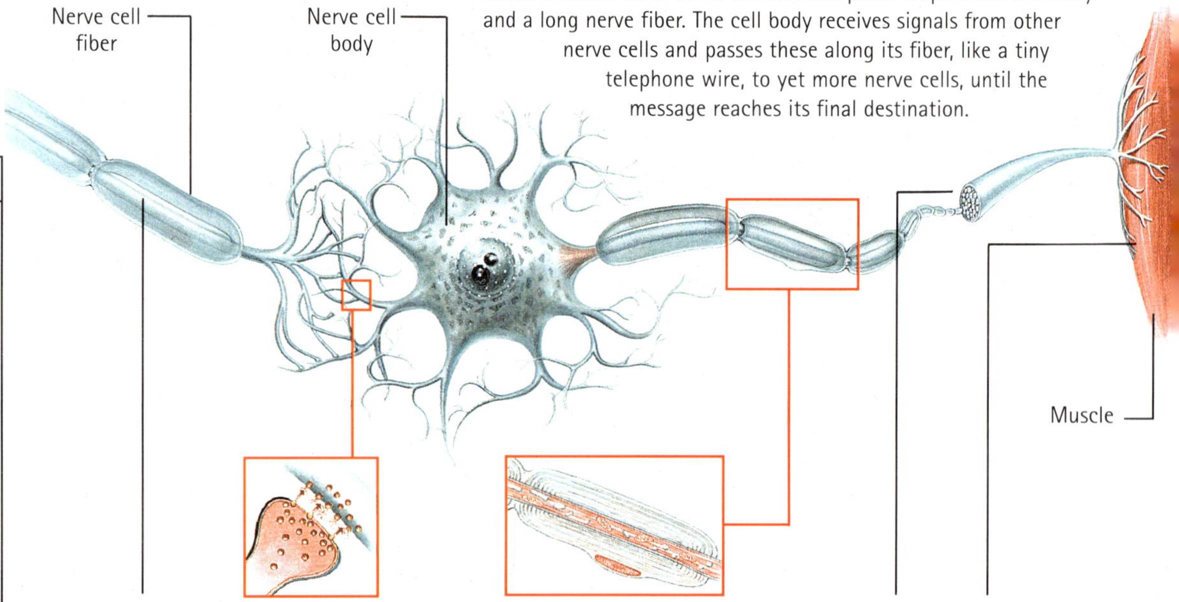

1 Messages are sent along a nerve fiber (axon) to another nerve cell.

2 The message has to jump the small gap (synapse) between the two nerve cells.

3 The message travels fast along the axon because it is insulated with a sheath of myelin.

4 The axon joins with other nerve fibers in a bundle, creating a pathway.

5 The muscle receives the message from the brain to move.

FAST FACTS

- About 1.9 pt. (0.85l) of blood pass through the brain every minute
- Brain activity uses one fifth of the body's energy supply
- The longest nerve, the sciatic, runs from the base of the spine to the knee. Nerve signals can travel at up to 250 mph (400kph)
- Meningitis is the inflammation of the meninges. Encephalitis is inflammation of the brain

THE BRAIN AND SKULL

The brain is protected by a bony skull, three thin layers of membrane, called meninges, and a pool of fluid. The two sides of the cerebrum (the cerebral hemispheres) are joined by the corpus callosum. The left side of the brain usually controls logic, and the right side is more active in creative pursuits.

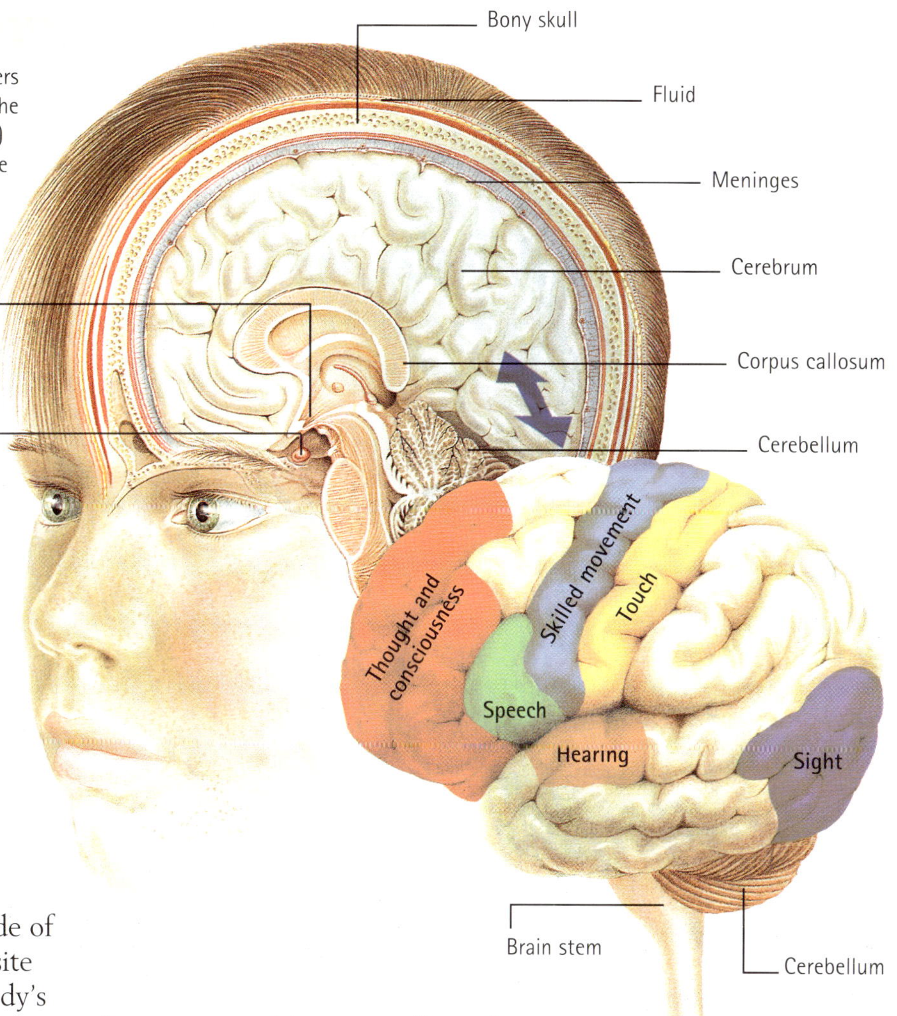

center, which sends nerve signals to the muscles. There are also areas for hearing, taste, speech, and other body processes. Consciousness and thought are believed to originate at the front of the cerebrum.

CROSSING THE DIVIDE

Nerve signals arriving or leaving one side of the brain cross over to affect the opposite side of the body, so signals from the body's right side go to the brain's left hemisphere and vice versa.The two sides are joined by a strip of nerve fibers, the corpus callosum.

INSTINCTS AND EMOTIONS

Basic instincts, such as hunger, thirst, and sleep, as well as strong emotions, such as fear, anger, and joy, come from the hypothalamus, which lies at the top of the brain stem. Dangling beneath it is the pituitary, a pea-size gland that controls the body's hormones (chemical messages).

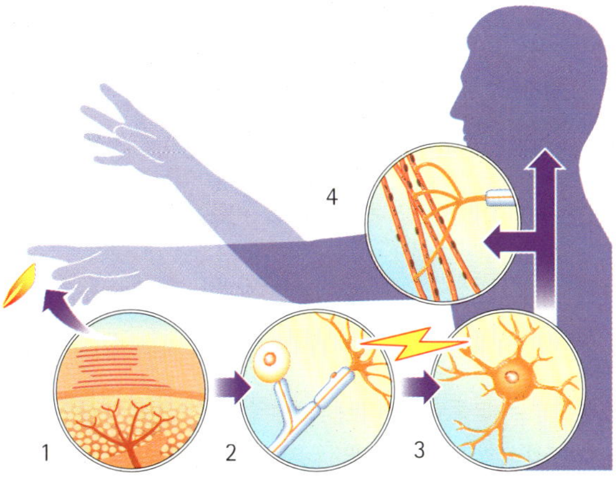

▲ A reflex is an automatic response. The flame's heat stimulates pain sensors in the finger (1) that send a signal to the spinal cord (2). The signal passes to a motor nerve (3), which makes muscles contract (4), pulling away the hand. Signals also pass to the brain, which registers pain.

THOUGHTS AND MEMORIES

The human brain contains 100 billion nerve cells and is far more complex than the most advanced supercomputer. One thought or memory involves millions of nerve signals, flashing around billions of brain cells, along trillions of pathways. An electroencephalogram (EEG) records these electrical nerve signals.

A NETWORK OF NERVES

The brain is linked to a branching network of nerves by the spinal cord. Sensory nerves bring information from the senses to the brain. Motor nerves carry signals from the brain to the muscles. The brain and spinal column make up the central nervous system. The nerves in the rest of the body make up the peripheral nervous system.

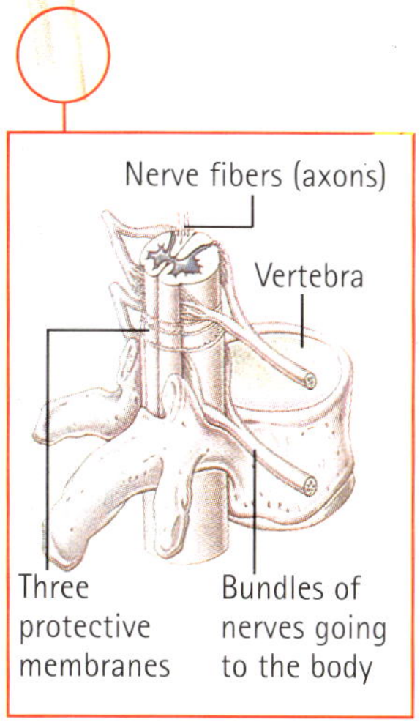

▲ The spinal cord runs through a tunnel formed by vertebrae in the spine. Its nerves are surrounded by protective membranes.

SEE ALSO

Cell, Gland, Hearing, Human body, Sight, Taste and smell, Touch

BRAZIL

Brazil is the largest country in South America, covering almost half the continent. It is also South America's richest and most heavily populated country.

Area: 3,286,169 sq. mi.
Population: 164 million
Capital: Brasilia
Language: Portuguese
Currency: Real

Two thirds of Brazil is covered by the Amazon River basin, which contains the world's largest rain forest. Some 3,900 mi. (6,276km) long, the Amazon flows across the northwest of the country and carries about a fifth of the world's river water.

ON THE EQUATOR

Brazil is warm all year round, with temperatures rarely dropping below 68°F (20°C), because the equator lies across the north of the country. Rainfall is highest inland, with more than 11 in. (280mm) of rain falling in January, the wettest month.

▲ São Paulo, Brazil's largest city, is ringed by shanty towns called *favelas*. Poverty is a serious problem for Brazil's rapidly growing population.

LIFE IN THE RAIN FOREST

The Amazon rain forest is a dense and steamy region, with at least 40,000 kinds of plants and thousands of different insects, exotic birds, and wild animals including macaws, monkeys, jaguars, sloths, armadillos, piranha fish, and anacondas. But the wildlife and the way of life of the small groups of Indians who inhabit the rain forest are under threat because of the number of trees being cut down. Efforts to protect the rain forest—an area of global environmental importance—are now being made. Farming, logging, and mining all threaten the region.

◀ Many families living in the heart of the Amazon rain forest still build their houses out of bamboo.

FARMING THE LAND

Most of Brazil's wealth comes from crops grown in mountainous areas. Coffee is the country's largest export—Brazil produces about a fifth of the world's supply. Other exports include orange juice, soybeans, rice, sugarcane, and cotton. Valuable timber, such as mahogany, as well as nuts, rubber, and medicines are harvested in the forests.

INDUSTRY AND MINING

Factories around the major cities make cars, aircraft, cement, and chemicals. Brazil's vast mineral wealth includes iron, lead, copper, magnesium, uranium, gold, and diamonds. Most of Brazil's power is hydroelectric, from projects such as the Itaipu Dam on the Paraná River at the Paraguay border.

▶ Sugarloaf Mountain overlooks the beautiful natural harbor of Rio de Janeiro, once the capital of Brazil. The mountain gets its name from the days when sugar was sold in pyramidlike, solid blocks.

▲ Each year, huge areas of forest are cleared for their timber and to make way for cattle ranches and roads. If this continues at the current rate, in 100 years there may be no rain forest at all left in Brazil.

▲ The Brazilian carnival lasts for five days just before Lent. It is especially spectacular in Rio de Janeiro.

WHERE PEOPLE LIVE

As many as 80 percent of Brazilians live in cities on the Atlantic coast and in the south. The best farming and mining areas, as well as the two biggest cities—São Paulo and Rio de Janeiro—are found there.

CULTURAL MIX

About 75 percent of Brazilians are of European origin, many with Portuguese ancestry. The rest are of mixed Indian, European, and African descent. Ancient settlers reached Brazil thousands of years ago; the Portuguese arrived in the 1500s, bringing African slaves with them. Brazil declared its independence from Portugal in 1822.

BRAZIL TODAY

Brazil is now a country of 27 states, each with its own local government. The country's capital, Brasilia, was built in the 1950s on the Central Plains to encourage development in inland areas of the country. Since the 1950s, Brazil's economic status in the world has grown, but at the expense of many of its natural resources. A third of Brazilians are under 15 years of age and the population is set to double before 2050. It is important that the country continues its economic growth if its population is to be housed, educated, and employed.

SEE ALSO

Conservation, Rain forest, South America, Sports

BRIDGE

Bridges are structures that are built to allow people, animals, or vehicles to cross rivers, canals, canyons, railroads, or roads.

Most bridges are fixed, but some are movable—all are designed to withstand the effects of traffic, floods, high winds, earthquakes, and temperature changes. The main types of fixed bridges in use today are truss, arch, suspension, and cantilever.

STRAIGHT ACROSS

The earliest bridges were simply logs or large, flat stones laid across a river. Truss or girder bridges take this idea further. They have a flat deck, sometimes supported by piers (pillars), and can span gaps of almost 1,000 ft. (300m). A cantilever bridge is a type of truss bridge with two halves balanced on piers and joined by a short span in the middle.

ARCH BRIDGES

Because of its curved shape, the arch bridge can reach farther than the truss bridge. Its supports at either end are called abutments. They take the strain of the outward thrust created by the weight of the arch. The Romans were the first to build arch bridges, using bricks or stone.

BRIDGES IN SUSPENSION

Suspension bridges can cover very long distances where piers cannot be used, perhaps because the river is too deep. The traffic deck is suspended from towers by steel cables. A modern version of this is the cable-stayed bridge, which does not need the heavy anchorages required to stabilize a suspension bridge.

MOVABLE BRIDGES

Some bridges are built to move so large ships can pass through them. Drawbridges lift up by splitting in the middle or at one end, swing bridges turn sideways, and lift bridges have a central section that can be raised. Deck sections can also be floated on pontoons to create temporary bridges.

◀ The 8,981 ft. (2,737m)-long Golden Gate suspension bridge in San Francisco hangs from two 3 ft. (1m)-thick suspension cables, each made of 27,450 wires.

HOW BRIDGES WORK

Bridges are designed to withstand huge forces (shown by the arrows in the diagrams below). They must be strong enough to carry their own weight, as well as that of the people and vehicles that use them. Bridges must also withstand the strong vibrations set up by high winds.

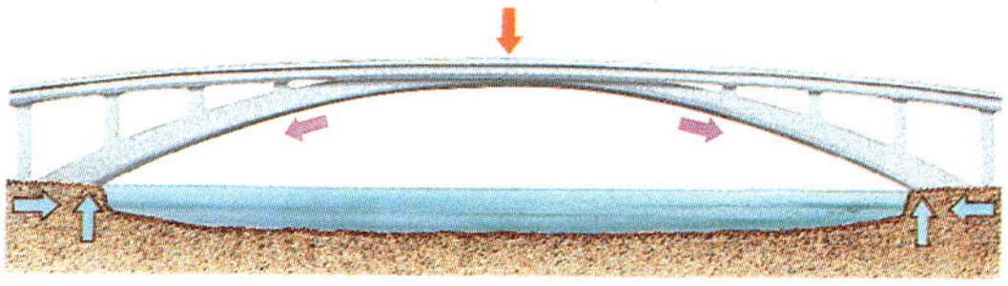

In an arch bridge, the downward pressure (load) is pushed out toward the foundations on each bank.

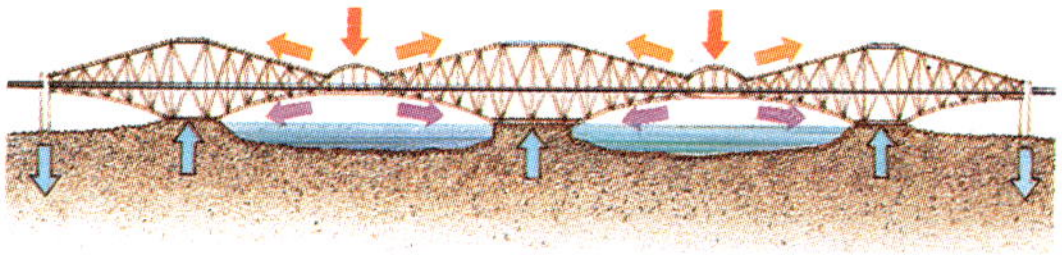

In a cantilever bridge, the load on the central span is balanced equally over each supporting pier.

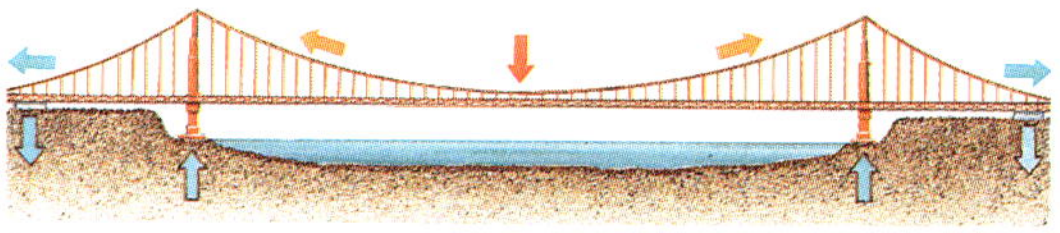

In a suspension bridge, curving cables transfer the bulk of the load to anchored points on each bank.

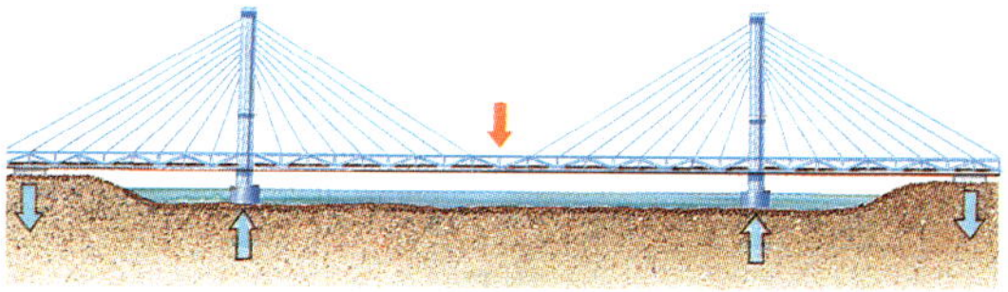

In a cable-stayed bridge, the load is balanced equally over one or more central supports.

→ Load → Support → Tension → Compression

SEE ALSO

Architecture, Construction, Industrial Revolution, Iron and steel

BUDDHISM

Buddhism is a religion that was first practiced in Asia about 2,500 years ago. Today, it is estimated that there are around 350 million Buddhists across the globe.

▲ The Wheel of Life symbolizes the process of change and rebirth. When we reach Nirvana, the process stops and we come off the wheel.

Buddhism was founded in northeast India by a prince called Siddhartha Gautama. Born around 563 B.C., he left his home at the age of 29 to lead a life of meditation and preaching. He became a great religious teacher before his death in about 483 B.C.

THE ENLIGHTENED ONE

While sitting under a fig tree, Gautama entered a peaceful state of mind called enlightenment—Nirvana ("absence of sorrow"). He taught others how to reach this state, and gained the title Buddha—"Enlightened One." The Buddhist religion spread from India to China, Japan, and other parts of Asia.

▲ A young Thai Buddhist monk, dressed in traditional orange robes, sits beside a prayer wheel. Written prayers attached to the wheel are recited as the wheel turns.

▲ A Buddhist monastery in Tibet. Buddhism was introduced into Tibet in A.D. 749. Tibetan monks are called lamas. The chief lamas are the Dalai Lama and the Panchen Lama.

REBIRTH

Buddhists believe in reincarnation—being reborn until Nirvana is reached. The form of each new life, or reincarnation, depends on how the being behaved during previous lives. A human might have been an animal in the last life; a male might have been a female. This is known as their karma.

FOUR NOBLE TRUTHS

Buddha's teachings are based on the Four Noble Truths. These state that all suffering is caused by attachment to the material world. Buddhists believe that they will be free of these attachments, and therefore of suffering, if they follow the Eightfold Path. This consists of eight steps involving wisdom, understanding, morality, and meditation.

TYPES OF BUDDHISM

There are two main types of Buddhism: Theravada is common in Southeast Asia and teaches that Buddha was an ordinary human being who achieved enlightenment; Mahayana is popular in northern Asia and claims that Buddha was the divine spirit in human form. A branch of Mahayana, called Zen Buddhism, was established in Japan in the 1100s.

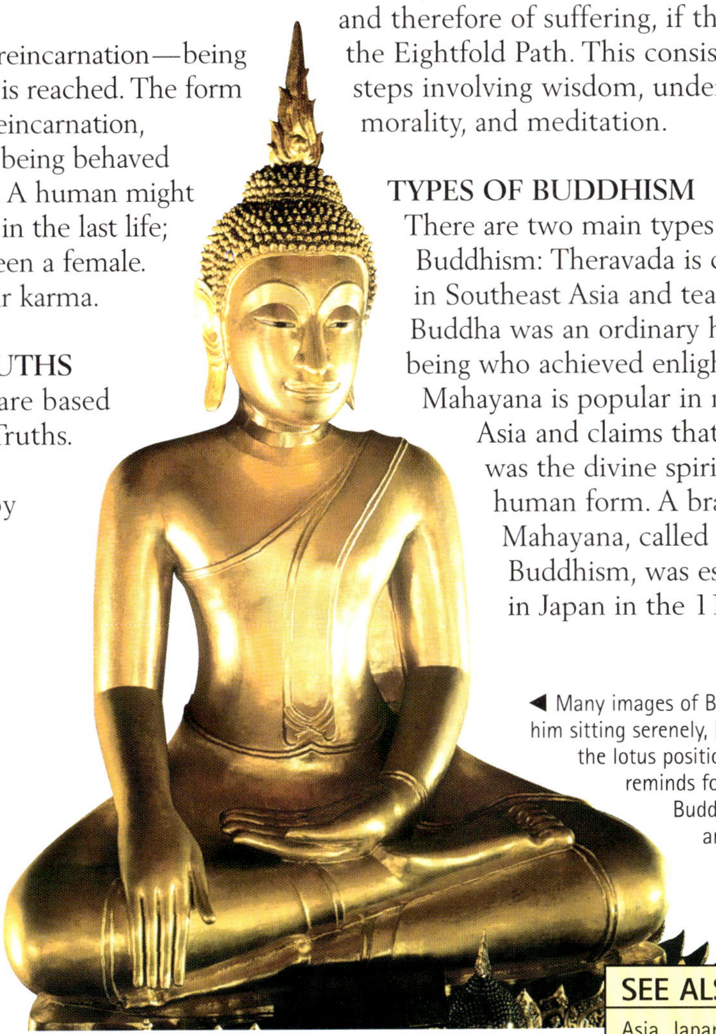

◀ Many images of Buddha show him sitting serenely, legs crossed in the lotus position. The image reminds followers of Buddha's goodness and helps them to meditate and pray.

EIGHTFOLD PATH TO ENLIGHTENMENT

- Right views
- Right thought and intention
- Right speech, plain and truthful
- Right action, including never taking a life
- Right occupation, harming no one
- Right effort, always persevering
- Right awareness of the past, present, and future
- Right contemplation or meditation

SEE ALSO
Asia, Japan, Religion

Butterfly and Moth

Butterflies and moths are flying insects with two pairs of wings, which are often brightly colored. They hatch as caterpillars and change into butterflies or moths as adults.

The turquoise blue has been hunted almost to extinction by collectors for its beautiful wings.

There are more than 170,000 kinds of butterflies and moths. They form the group of insects known as Lepidoptera, which means "scale wing." Their wings are covered with thousands of tiny scales that give the wings their colorful appearance.

▲ Tropical birdwing butterflies, such as the Rajah Brooke, can have a wingspan of 12 inches.

COLORFUL BUTTERFLIES

Most butterflies fly by day and have brightly colored wings that close together over their backs when they are resting. They have a slim body and thin antennae (feelers) with clubbed tips, which are used to detect smells. The monarch, cabbage white, tortoiseshell, and peacock are all types of butterfly.

DULL MOTHS

Most moths are dull in color, fly at night, have feathery or hairy antennae and a stout and hairy body. At rest, a moth holds its wings open. A moth's forewing is often linked to its hindwing on each side by tiny hairs that act like hooks. The hawkmoth, ermine, eggar, and tussock are all types of moth. The scarlet tiger and burnet are examples of moths that are brightly colored and fly by day.

EGG TO CATERPILLAR

After mating, female butterflies and moths lay their eggs on or near the plant that their caterpillars like to eat. The brimstone butterfly likes buckthorn; the green oak tortrix moth chooses oak leaves. Some species will feed only on one type of plant.

A peacock butterfly's eye spots may help it scare off small birds when it suddenly opens its wings.

The white admiral is a woodland butterfly. Its caterpillar is covered with protective spines.

Swallowtails are large and colorful butterflies found in North Africa, Europe, and across Asia.

The large white is a very common butterfly. Its caterpillars feed in groups, often on cabbage plants.

CATERPILLAR TO BUTTERFLY

The monarch butterfly lays its eggs on a milkweed plant. A week later, a caterpillar emerges from each egg. First it eats its egg case, then it feeds on the plant. Once fully grown, the caterpillar becomes a chrysalis (pupa). Inside, it metamorphoses (changes form) before emerging as a butterfly. The whole cycle from egg to adult takes about five weeks.

1 The female monarch lays a cluster of eggs on the leaves of a milkweed plant.

2 Each tiny caterpillar (larva) hatches and starts to eat. It grows quickly.

3 When fully grown, the caterpillar spins a silken thread and firmly attaches itself to a twig.

4 The caterpillar sheds its striped skin, revealing a chrysalis (pupa). It now looks still and lifeless.

LIVING TO EAT

Butterfly and moth eggs hatch into soft-skinned, wingless larvae called caterpillars. Their job is to eat—a large group of caterpillars can destroy crops within a few weeks. A caterpillar sheds its skin (molts) four or five times as it feeds and grows.

ALL CHANGE

When they are ready to become adults, caterpillars enter a pupal stage (chrysalis). Many moth caterpillars spin cocoons of silk around themselves. Butterfly caterpillars grow hard skins. Inside these cases, they gradually change. After a few weeks, or the following spring, the chrysalis splits and the adult winged insect (imago) emerges.

LIFE SPAN

Most butterflies and nearly all moths live for just one breeding season or year. A few, such as peacock and monarch butterflies, survive the winter as adults. Their main predators are birds by day and bats at night. Breeding time is usually spring or summer, although tropical species can breed at any time of the year.

SENSING THE WORLD

An adult butterfly or moth sees well with its large eyes. Its antennae pick up the scents of flowers and fruits and can detect the smell of a mate. Most species feed on flower nectar, which is sucked up by a long, strawlike mouth called a proboscis.

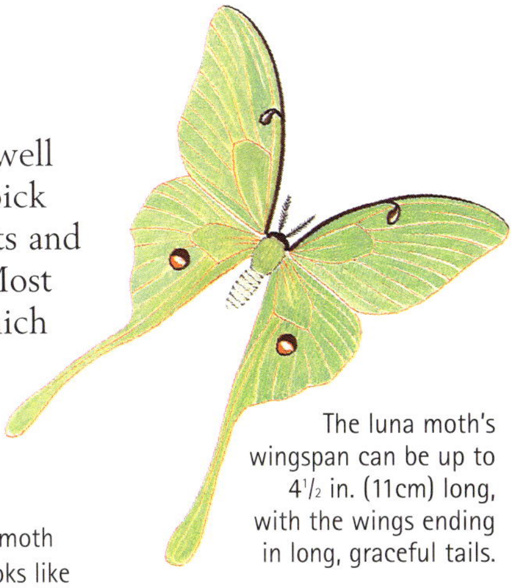

The luna moth's wingspan can be up to $4^1/_2$ in. (11cm) long, with the wings ending in long, graceful tails.

◀ This hawkmoth caterpillar looks like a viper in order to deceive predators into leaving it alone.

▼ This peppered moth is colored a pale, speckled gray to camouflage it against lichen on tree bark.

The bright colors of the tiger moth, which is covered in hairs, warn birds that it is unpleasant to eat.

Like all hawkmoths, the privet hawkmoth is a fast flyer. Its caterpillars have a curved horn at the end.

5 Inside the chrysalis a new body slowly forms. Finally, the skin splits and an adult butterfly emerges.

6 The butterfly clings to the twig, letting its new wings hang down to help force blood into them.

7 When the wings have dried and hardened, metamorphosis is complete and the adult monarch butterfly can fly away.

Death's-head hawkmoths are named after the strange markings on the upper part of their body.

The elephant hawkmoth's bright coloring helps to hide it as it feeds among honeysuckle flowers.

SEE ALSO

Animal, Flower, Insect

CANADA

Canada is the second largest country in the world. It lies at the top of the continent of North America and a large percentage of its area lies within the Arctic Circle.

Area: 3,851,809 sq. mi.
Population: 29,123,194
Capital: Ottawa
Languages: English, French
Currency: Canadian dollar

▲ Forestry is one of Canada's most important industries. Trees are cut down to make paper as well as to build homes.

FAST FACTS

- The Yukon Territory is rich in metal ore. During the 1890s, it was the site of the Klondike gold rush
- Alberta has some of the world's best dinosaur remains. *Albertosaurus* is just one example
- The Canadian–U.S. border is the longest undefended border in the world

The Rocky Mountains run down the west of Canada, and four of the five Great Lakes lie on its border with the United States. These, together with other Canadian lakes, contain about a fourth of the world's fresh water.

CANADIAN FORESTS

Forests cover 40 percent of the country. British Columbia is the leading province in timber production, with 250 ft. (75m)-high trees, such as Douglas fir, growing in its moist, coniferous forests. Maple syrup is collected in the forests in Ontario and Quebec, and in the southwest there are orchards and vineyards.

THE GREAT PLAINS

Canada has vast grassland areas, or prairies, stretching across its center. Only about seven percent of Canada's land is used for growing crops, but these fertile plains produce enough to make Canada the world's second largest exporter of wheat. Cattle ranches on the drier grasslands supply beef and dairy produce.

▲ Moose are just one of the animals living in Canada's forests, which are also home to bears, beavers, bobcats, caribou, foxes, wolves, mountain lions, and goats.

INDUSTRY AND MINING

Manufacturing industries lie mostly in Ontario and Quebec. Products include cars, trucks, aircraft, machinery, steel, paper, and chemicals, as well as processed food and minerals. Among Canada's resources are gold, iron ore, copper, petroleum, and natural gas. Fishing is important, but overfishing has greatly reduced stocks.

SPORTS AND LEISURE

Most Canadians share a love of the outdoors, enjoying baseball, football, soccer, skiing, and ice skating. Competitive ice hockey is usually played indoors. Rodeo enthusiasts flock to the annual Calgary Stampede. There are over 30 national parks.

◀ In wintertime, temperatures can fall as low as –22°F (–30°C). Lakes and rivers freeze over, and people play games on the ice.

▶ The 1,814 ft. (553m)-high Canadian National (CN) Tower dominates Toronto's skyline. The city is Canada's financial, manufacturing, and communication center.

◀ Canada's Horseshoe Falls is one of the two waterfalls that make up Niagara Falls.

▲ The Royal Canadian Mounted Police, nicknamed the Mounties, are Canada's national police force.

CANADIAN PEOPLE

The ancestors of Canada's Native Americans arrived from Asia at least 13,500 years ago—possibly much longer. Those of the Inuit arrived much later and are not related to the earlier settlers. Europeans arrived during the 1500s. From 1754 to 1763, in the French and Indian War, Britain fought France for control of its Canadian territory (New France) and won. Since 1867, the country has been self-governing. Newfoundland became part of Canada in 1947.

THE GOVERNMENT

Canada is divided into ten provinces and two territories. The provinces make their own laws, but the territories are mainly under government control. National laws are made by an elected parliament that is located in Ottawa. There is also an unelected body of senators; they act as consultants and advise parliament.

TRANSPORTATION

Canada has a good system of roads, including the Trans-Canada Highway, which is more than 4,350 mi. (7,000km) long. The St. Lawrence Seaway, a waterway linking stretches of rivers and canals, allows ships to carry cargoes inland from the Atlantic Ocean as far as the Great Lakes.

SEE ALSO

Arctic, Grassland, Native American, North America

CAR

Cars are motorized vehicles with an engine, wheels, and steering mechanism. They are designed to carry passengers or to race in competitions.

Cugnot's steam gun carriage of 1769 was the first motorized vehicle.

Daimler's first car, built in 1886, was a coach fitted with an engine.

The Rolls Royce Silver Ghost of 1906 used automatic engine controls.

The 1914 Model T Ford was the first car made on a moving assembly line.

Over 20 million Volkswagen Beetles have been sold since 1938.

The 1984 Ferrari Testarossa can reach a speed of 180 mph (290kph).

The General Motors Sunraycer uses solar energy from sunlight.

There are over 400 million cars on the road today. They have had a huge impact on society and are one of the world's most important inventions.

THE FIRST CARS

The first successful gasoline (gas)-powered vehicles were developed by the German engineers Karl Benz and Gottfried Daimler in the 1880s. Benz designed a complete vehicle. Daimler simply added his engine to a horseless carriage.

HOW A CAR MOVES

Most cars today are powered by gas or diesel engines, or by electric motors. The engine turns a driveshaft, which is linked to the wheels by gears.

▲ Racing cars are designed to have minimum air resistance. They have a sleek shape and pointed nose.

STREAMLINING

A car's shape is now designed using computers. It must look good, be safe and comfortable, and work well. The sleeker or more streamlined the car, the faster and more economical it will be to drive. Objects that stick out, such as windshield wipers, can be hidden under panels to reduce wind resistance and wind noise. In some modern designs, front and rear panels on the car can be adjusted electronically to change the airflow around the car's body.

CONTROL SYSTEMS

Gearboxes have up to five forward gears to vary the speed and power of the car, and one gear for reversing. Gears are selected by a shift lever, although many gearboxes are automatic. An electrical system controls the engine, lights, and other instruments. The electric circuits are powered by a battery, which is charged from the engine. Computerized engine management systems in modern cars make it easier for problems to be diagnosed.

ROAD SAFETY

Road safety is very important in the design of modern cars. Experiments using life-size dummies examine how a car collapses on impact and how this affects the passengers inside. These experiments have led to improvements in the design of the steering wheel, seats, and seat belts, and to safety devices such as inflatable air bags.

IMPROVING COMFORT

Passenger comfort is improved by smooth braking and suspension. Brakes are linked to all four wheels to slow the car down. Modern cars use antilocking brakes to prevent skidding when roads are wet or slippery. The suspension system cushions the car from bumps in the road and usually consists of a coiled spring and shock absorber (to reduce the spring's vibrations) attached to each of the four wheels.

THE ENVIRONMENT

Cars have caused huge environmental and social changes, bringing mobility to millions of people. Thousands of miles of expressways have been built, and the ability to travel long distances to work has helped towns to spread. However, poisonous gases from car exhausts and traffic congestion do cause serious problems. It is hoped that the use of new fuels, such as methanol or hydrogen, as well as electric motors, will reduce this pollution.

KEY DATES

1891 René Panhard and Emile Levasor build first "horseless" carriage powered by a Daimler engine

1896 Karl Benz patents first automobile

1901 First mass-produced car, the Oldsmobile, is produced by Ransom Eli Olds in the United States

1906 First Grand Prix held at Le Mans, France

1908 Henry Ford introduces the Model T

1934 André Citroën introduces front-wheel drive

1979 Catalytic converter is introduced

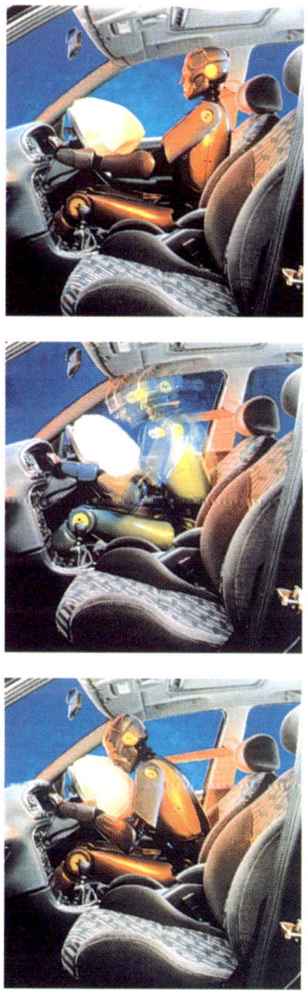

▲ Crash test dummies are used to test cars for road safety. Here an air bag is shown exploding after a crash. The dummy mimics how a person would be affected in the accident.

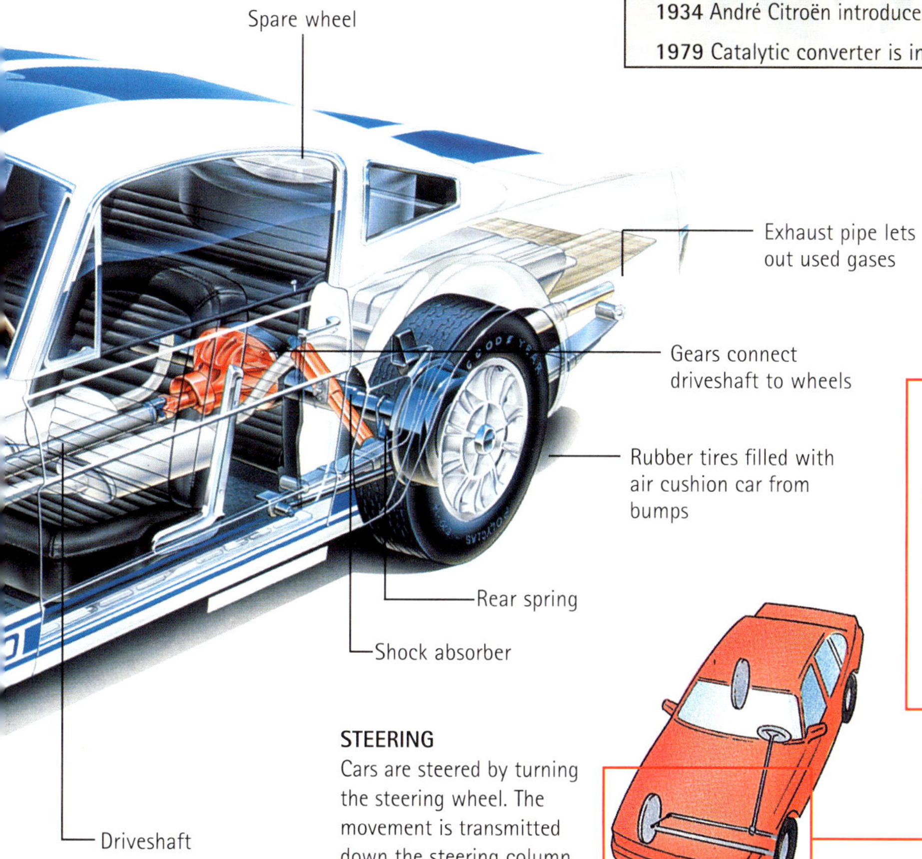

STEERING

Cars are steered by turning the steering wheel. The movement is transmitted down the steering column to a rack and pinion. As the rack moves, it moves track rods linked to the front wheels. Some cars can steer all four wheels.

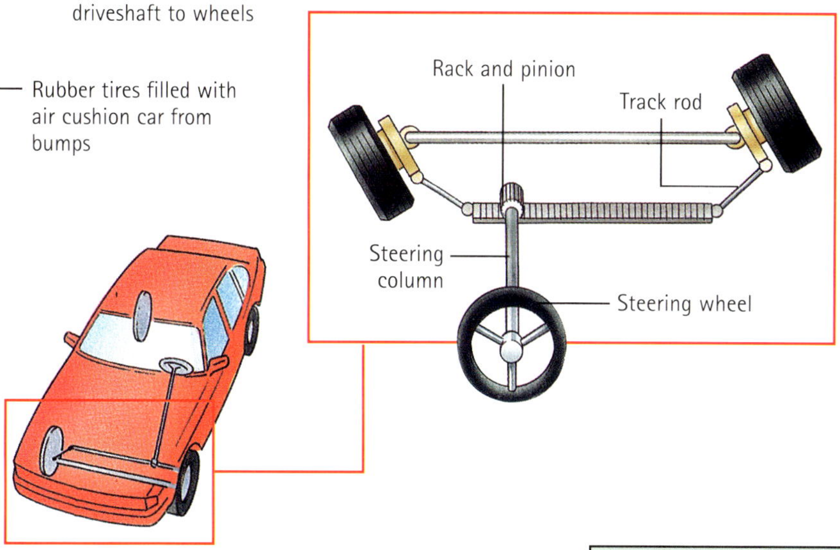

SEE ALSO

Invention, Transportation, Truck and bus

CARIBBEAN

The Caribbean islands lie between North and South America, forming a chain about 2,000 mi. (3,200km) long. They include Cuba, Jamaica, and Haiti.

ANTIGUA & BARBUDA
Area: 275 sq. mi.
Population: 77,000
Capital: St. John's
Language: English
Currency: East Caribbean dollar

BAHAMAS
Area: 4,404 sq. mi.
Population: 262,034
Capital: Nassau
Language: English
Currency: Bahamian dollar

BARBADOS
Area: 116 sq. mi.
Population: 257,731
Capital: Bridgetown
Language: English
Currency: East Caribbean dollar

CUBA
Area: 46,736 sq. mi.
Population: 10,999,041
Capital: Havana
Language: Spanish
Currency: Peso

DOMINICA
Area: 305 sq. mi.
Population: 83,226
Capital: Roseau
Language: English
Currency: East Caribbean dollar

The region known as the Caribbean includes three island groups: the Greater Antilles and the Lesser Antilles, which lie in the Caribbean Sea, and the Bahamas, in the Atlantic Ocean. These islands are also known as the West Indies because, when the explorer Christopher Columbus first saw them in 1492, he believed he was near India.

TROPICAL ISLANDS

The Caribbean's tropical climate and steady ocean winds mean that temperatures rarely drop below 77°F (25°C), although the hot days are often relieved by cooling sea breezes. Violent hurricanes sometimes strike the islands, causing great damage to property and crops.

FOREST ANIMALS

Vegetation on the islands includes palm trees and exotic flowers such as orchids. Some islands also have very dense rain forests—home to parrots and macaws, as well as bats, snakes, and insects. In many places, these forests have been cleared to make way for crop plantations.

▼ Large markets, where people sell homegrown goods, are a familiar aspect of island life.

▲ Bananas are one of the chief crops. They are picked while still green and exported in refrigerated cargo ships.

HOMEGROWN PRODUCE

Sugarcane is the main crop grown on the islands. Stalks are crushed for raw juice or refined to make crystallized sugar. Bananas and other fruits are important crops, as are coffee, cocoa, and cotton.

ISLAND INDUSTRY

As well as farming, there is some mining on the islands. Jamaica has bauxite (aluminum ore), and there is gold in the Dominican Republic. Cuba, Trinidad, and Barbados all have offshore oil and gas, and there is some manufacturing. Tourism is the largest industry, employing as many as one in five people on many of the islands.

THE ORIGINAL ISLANDERS

The first settlers in the Caribbean were the Caribs and Arawaks from South America. Most were killed by Europeans who arrived

DOMINICAN REPUBLIC
Area: 18,700 sq. mi.
Population: 8,228,151
Capital: Santo Domingo
Language: Spanish
Currency: Peso

GRENADA
Area: 133 sq. mi.
Population: 95,537
Capital: St. George's
Language: English
Currency: East Caribbean dollar

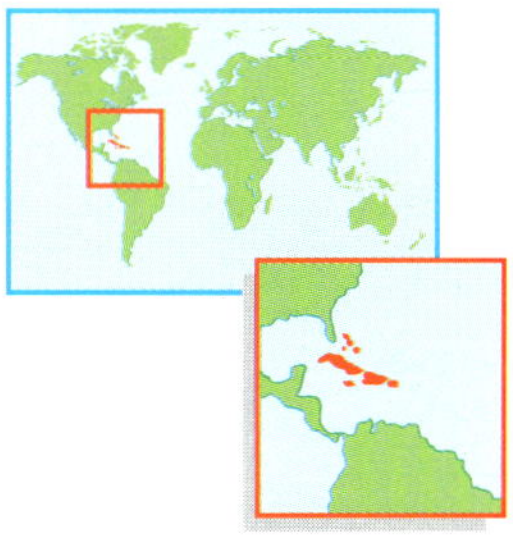

HAITI
Area: 16,714 sq. mi.
Population: 6,611,407
Capital: Port-au-Prince
Language: French
Currency: Gourde

JAMAICA
Area: 4,411 sq. mi.
Population: 2,615,582
Capital: Kingston
Language: English
Currency: Jamaican dollar

KEY TO MAP
1 VIRGIN IS. (U.S.)
2 VIRGIN IS. (U.K.)
3 ANGUILLA (U.K.)

Countries in parentheses are countries of which that island or group is a dependency. Aruba (Netherlands) is not shown.

◀ This square in Cuba has architecture typical of that built by the European colonials.

soon after Columbus sighted the islands. The Europeans brought slaves from Africa to work on sugar and cotton plantations. After the abolition of slavery in the 1800s, people from India and China came to work in the Caribbean.

A CULTURAL MIX

The people of the Caribbean reflect its mix of cultures. They speak Spanish, French, or English, often with a local dialect. Religion is an important part of life. As well as Christians, Hindus, and Muslims, there are Rastafarians, who worship Haile Selassie (emperor of Ethiopia until 1974) as a god. On Haiti, many people practice voodoo, a blend of African and Christian beliefs.

SELF-GOVERNING

Most larger islands are self-governing. Others are dependencies still linked to a colonial partner. They include Guadeloupe (France) and the two Virgin Island groups (U.K. and U.S.). The governments of the Caribbean are working to develop the islands, many of which are poor. In the last 50 years, many islanders have migrated to Britain, Canada, or the U.S. to find work.

ST. KITTS-NEVIS
Area: 152 sq. mi.
Population: 41,803
Capital: Basseterre
Language: English
Currency: East Caribbean dollar

ST. LUCIA
Area: 233 sq. mi.
Population: 159,639
Capital: Castries
Language: English
Currency: East Caribbean dollar

▲ The beautiful sandy beaches and warm waters of the Caribbean islands lure tourists from all over the world.

ST. VINCENT & THE GRENADINES
Area: 150 sq. mi.
Population: 119,092
Capital: Kingstown
Language: English
Currency: East Caribbean dollar

TRINIDAD & TOBAGO
Area: 1,864 sq. mi.
Population: 1,273,141
Capital: Port of Spain
Language: English
Currency: Trinidad dollar

SEE ALSO
Empire, Explorer, North America, Slavery

CARTOON AND ANIMATION

A cartoon can be an animated film, a comic strip, or a single picture. The first cartoons, in the 1840s, ridiculed prominent people or political events.

©Disney

Mickey Mouse, created in 1928, is a traditional hand-drawn character.

©Aardman Animation

Wallace and Gromit films are made with clay models.

©Disney

Toy Story used 3-D models created on a computer.

The word "cartoon" was originally used by artists to describe the picture they produced as part of the preparation for a painting or tapestry. Today, cartoons are seen on screen and in print.

CEL ANIMATION

The traditional way of making cartoons for TV and film involves creating a moving sequence from a collection of individual images. This is known as cel animation. Each action or change of expression of a character is made by using a number of slightly different hand-drawn pictures. When shown one after another on film, these give the illusion of movement.

A CAST OF THOUSANDS

A 20-minute animated film needs between 15,000 and 20,000 images, so a longer film needs a whole studio of artists. Painters create a background for each scene, illustrators draw the characters, then other artists touch up the lines; Disney's *Beauty and the Beast* had 90 such artists.

◄ Spiderman, created in 1962, has crossed over from comic book to animated film.

©Marvel Comics

Once the image has been colored, it is placed on a clear plastic sheet of celluloid, or cellulose acetate, by a paint and trace artist and then shot onto film.

COMPUTER ANIMATION

Many artists still draw by hand and use computers to add color and speed up rendering (planning the movements and creating the frames). Disney's *Toy Story*, made in 1995, was the first full-length film made entirely by computer animation.

COMIC STRIPS

Comic strips use a smaller creative team than animated films. A strip tells a story in a series of pictures. Speech balloons are used to put words into the mouths of characters.

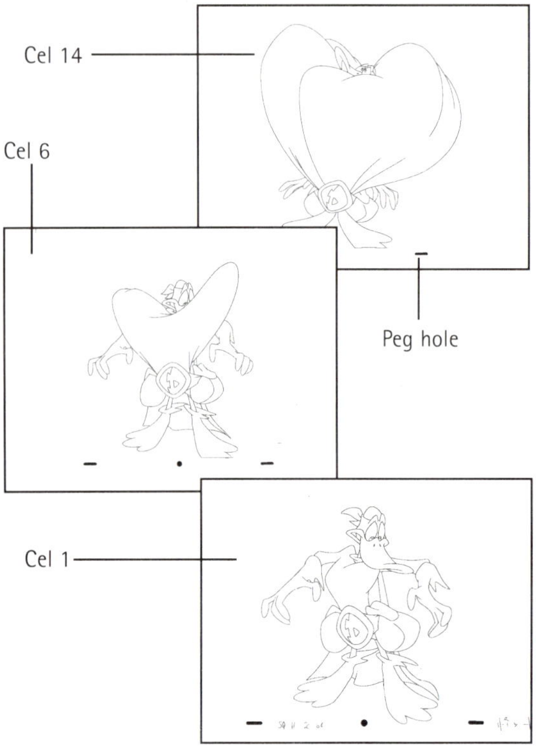

COMPUTER EFFECTS

In *The Duck* by Uli Meyer Animation, the figures were hand-drawn on transparent plastic, then scanned into a computer to be colored in and made three-dimensional. About 750 drawings were used in a five-second scene where Duck foils two robbers. The drawings (cels) are pegged one over the other to check the order of movement.

SEE ALSO

Computer, Design, Film, Newspaper and magazine

Castle

Castles are fortified homes that were owned by rich and powerful families during the Middle Ages. Some are still in use, but many are now in ruins.

Early castles, known as motte and baileys, were made of wood and soil.

Massive stone keeps began to be erected around 1070.

Concentric castles had two or more walls and strongly guarded gatehouses.

In the Middle Ages, castles were used to protect towns, river crossings, and frontiers. They were also used to guard against invasion and prevent rebellion.

MOTTE AND BAILEY

Castles were first built around A.D. 950 by knights or lords. The castles included a hill or mound surrounded by a ditch and topped by a wooden tower called a motte. A bailey, or courtyard, contained living quarters, stables, granaries, and barns. These early castles were protected by a high wooden fence, called a palisade.

STONE CASTLES

From about 1070, larger castles had a stone tower called a keep. The Tower of London, the first keep in England, was begun in 1078. Food and weapons were stored inside the tower, and the knight and his staff lived there. Prisoners were kept in dungeons.

TOWERS AND WALLS

From the 1100s onward, stone curtain walls were built to surround the keeps. Towers were added to the outside of the walls so that attackers could be shot at from different directions. After about 1270, a second outer wall was added to some castles to make them harder to attack. These castles, often built by Crusaders in the Middle East, were called concentric because of their double walls.

UNDER ATTACK

A castle was attacked with catapults, rams, and siege towers. Boulders and flaming missiles were hurled at it, and its walls undermined. If a castle was not captured quickly it was besieged. Most castles fell because of bribery, disease, or famine.

CANNON FIRE

By the 1450s, cannons and gunpowder became powerful enough to destroy walls. Castles were no longer safe from attack. Most fell into ruin, but some continued to be used as palaces or luxurious homes.

UNDER SIEGE

Armies attacked castles by smashing walls with catapults or rams and by digging out foundations so that the walls collapsed. The moat was drained and filled in so that siege machines could be wheeled right up to the walls. Attackers were shielded by frames covered with wet hides.

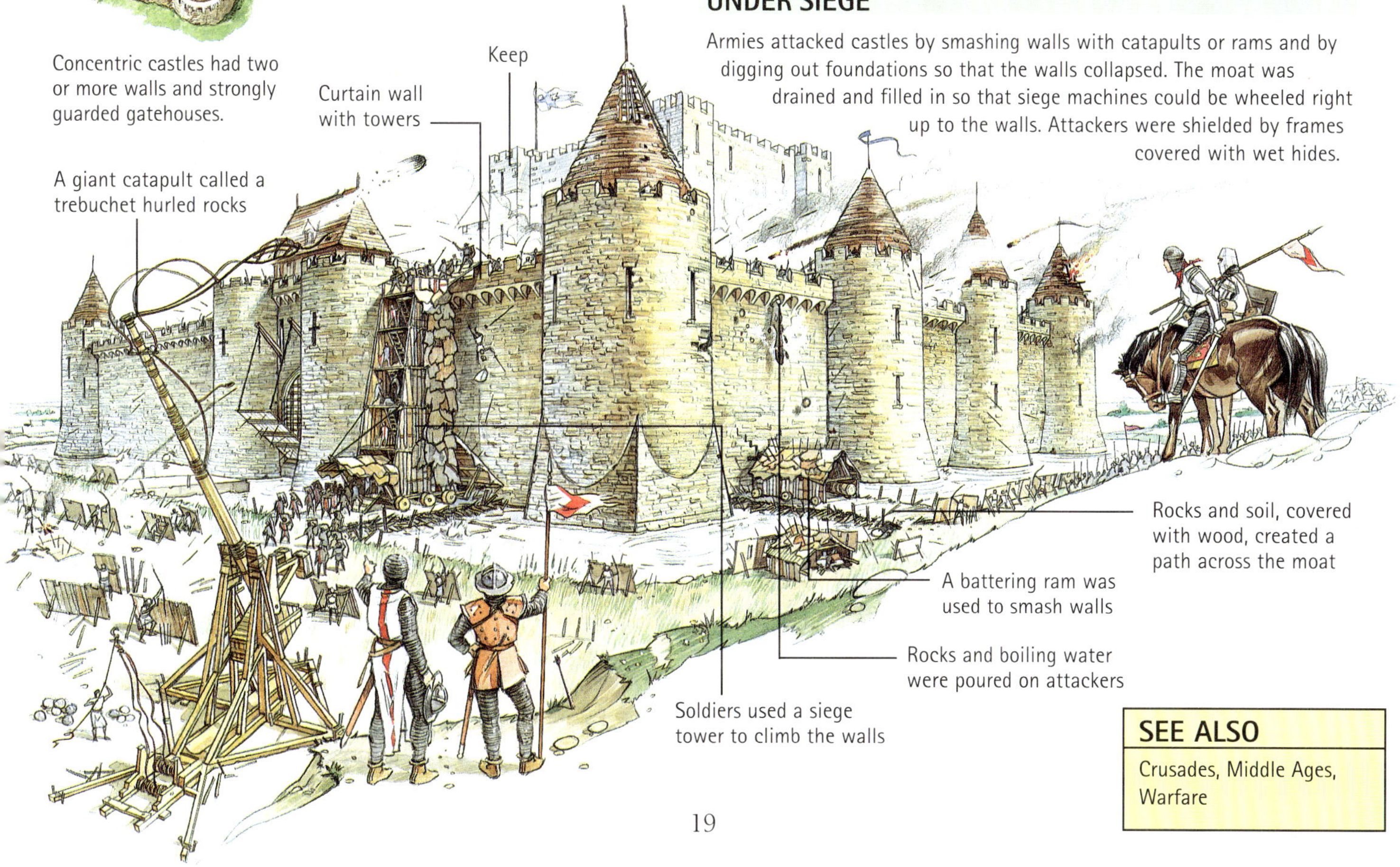

SEE ALSO
Crusades, Middle Ages, Warfare

CAT

Cats are agile, hunting mammals with keen senses and sharp teeth and claws. Domestic cats make some of the most popular pets.

The longhaired Persian needs regular grooming to keep its coat sleek.

The hairless sphinx was bred in the 1960s from a kitten born without fur.

The Manx cat from the Isle of Man, in the U.K., is famous for its lack of a tail.

The blue shorthair has copper eyes and a quiet, affectionate nature.

The Cornish rex has a curly coat of short, thin hair and large, open ears.

The Siamese has long been one of the most popular pedigreed (purebred) cats.

HUNTER IN THE HOME

Even a domestic cat, like this tabby, has the hunting instincts of its wild relations. Cats often toy with their prey, rather than killing it immediately. They hunt mostly at night, catching mice, small birds, and insects.

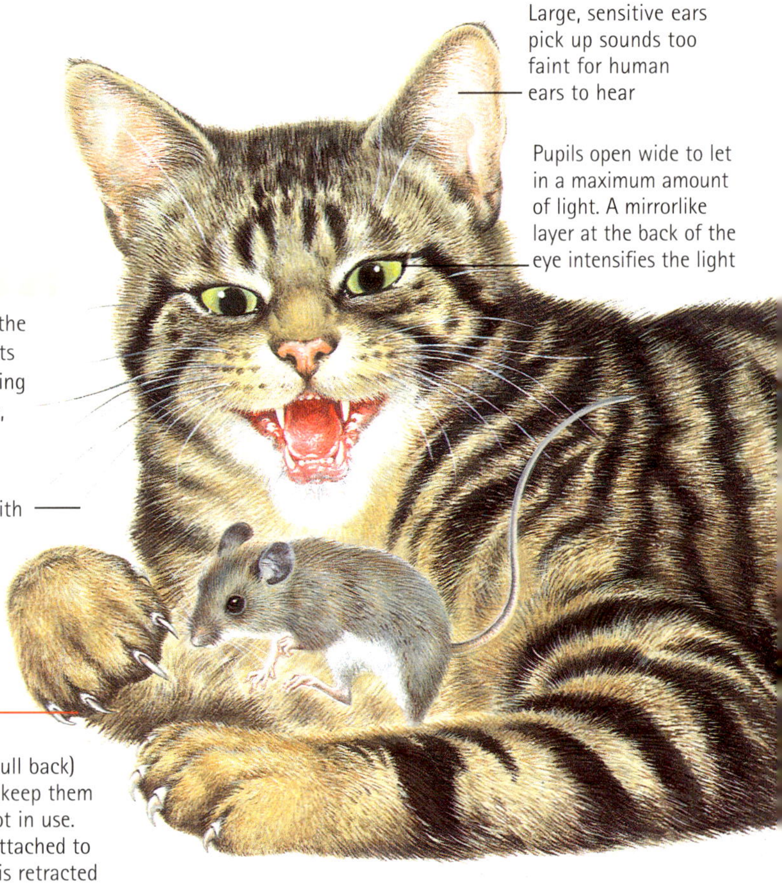

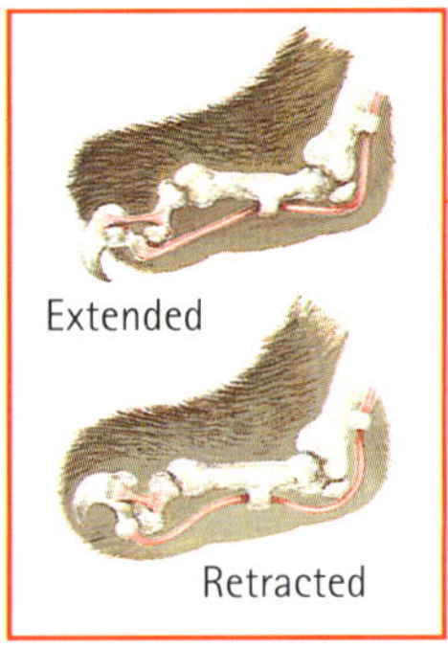

THE CLAWS

Cats retract (pull back) their claws to keep them sharp when not in use. Each claw is attached to a toe bone. It is retracted by ligaments, which are worked by muscles.

The cat family is divided into two main groups, based largely on size. The first group is made up of big cats such as tigers, lions, and leopards. The second includes cougars, bobcats, and lynxes, as well as the many small wild cats and the domestic cat. In all there are about 37 species of cat.

PET CATS

It is thought that the domestic cat was originally a small wild cat living in Africa. By 2000 B.C. it had been tamed by the Ancient Egyptians, who used it to protect their stored food from mice and rats. Today, there are many breeds of domestic cat, including longhaired Persians and Angoras and the shorthaired Manx and Siamese.

CAT CHARACTERISTICS

Domestic cats resemble their wild relatives in many ways. They are excellent hunters, strong and agile, with a keen sense of hearing and very good eyesight. They have curved claws, strong jaws, sharp teeth, and whiskers that are sensitive to touch. Cats are naturally inquisitive and are expert climbers and jumpers. Their flexible backbones allow them to swivel their bodies into a wide range of positions.

CAT BEHAVIOR

Cats spend at least an hour a day grooming their fur by licking it with their rough tongues. This helps to keep their fur in good condition and keeps them cool in hot weather. Cats sleep, on the average, twice as long as other mammals, spending up to three fourths of the day asleep, usually in short intervals—hence "catnaps."

HUNTING TACTICS

Although most domestic cats do not have to catch their own food, their instinct (inborn behavior) is to hunt. A cat's sensitive nose quickly picks up the scent of its prey. With its soft, padded paws, a cat can stalk its prey without being noticed until it is close enough to pounce. Then it grabs the prey with its claws and kills it with a powerful bite—usually at the back of the head, breaking the victim's neck.

SEE ALSO
Animal, Mammal, Sight, Tiger

Cave

Caves are hollows that are formed in rock and ice by erosion (wearing away), usually by water. The largest, most impressive caves are found in limestone rock.

Some caves consist of just one hole barely large enough for a person to enter; others are intricate mazes of passageways and chambers. The Mammoth Cave network in Kentucky is the world's longest. Its labyrinth of caves stretches for 350 mi. (560km).

ROCK, ICE, AND LAVA

Caves sometimes form in sea cliffs, where waves attack weak spots in the rock. The pressure of the water and the salty spray gradually erode the cliff structures. Long, tunnel-like caves can also develop in glaciers where streams of melted water run beneath the ice. Similar caves can be found in volcanoes, where a crust forms over a liquid stream of molten lava.

LIMESTONE CAVES

The largest and most impressive caves are found in limestone rock, where rainwater (which is slightly acidic) trickles through cracks in the rock. The rock slowly dissolves and the thin cracks get wider and wider. The trickle of rainwater swells into a stream, which carves hollows in the stone to form caves and potholes.

THE INSIDE STORY

Where streams meet, they carve out very large caves, or caverns. The floor of the cavern may be filled by underground lakes, so that it can only be explored by diving. Water dripping from the ceilings of limestone caves is rich in minerals, such as calcium carbonate, from the dissolved rock. As the water drips, these minerals are often deposited in dramatic columns—long, slender stalactites hang down from the ceiling; shorter, stumpier stalagmites grow up from the floor. Where they join together, a pillar is formed.

MAKING CAVES

It takes thousands of years for a limestone cave to form. The process begins when rainwater starts to wear away the stone and seep through cracks. Horizontal caverns are made where the water forms underground lakes. These are left dry when the level of groundwater falls.

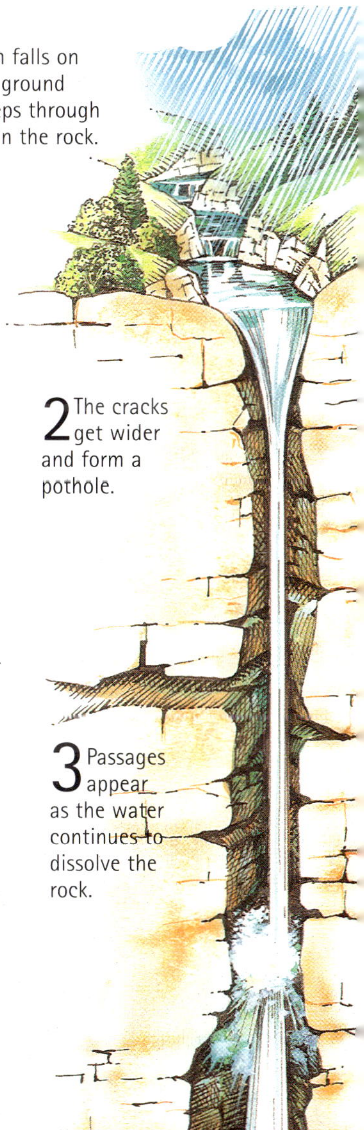

SEE ALSO

Glacier, Rock, Seashore, Volcano, Water

CELL

Cells are the smallest units capable of all the functions of life. Some living things are single cells; others (such as ourselves) are made up of billions of cells.

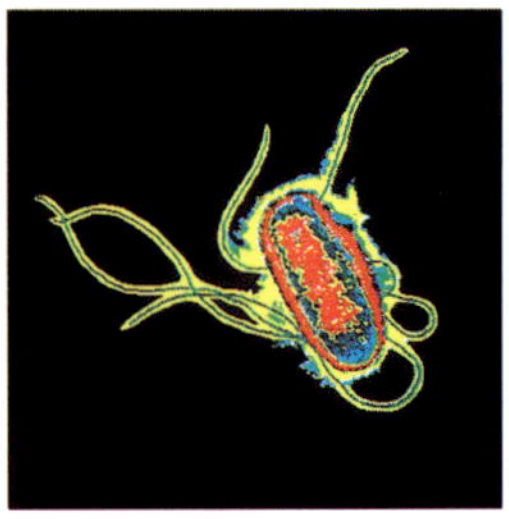

Bacteria have only one cell and can multiply fast.

Onions, like most plants, have box-shaped cells.

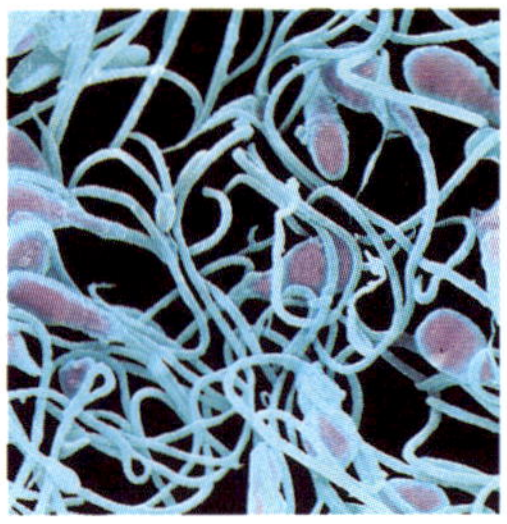

Sperm cells are used in reproduction.

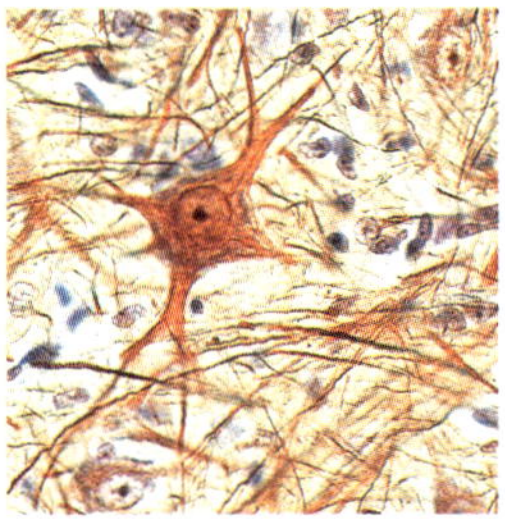

Nerve cells take messages to and from the brain.

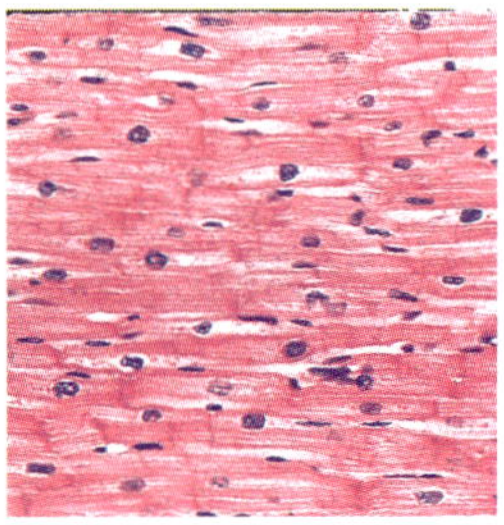

Muscle cells are long and thin and lie in bundles.

Every living thing is made up of tiny chambers, called cells—the basic building blocks of all organisms. Every cell has its job, but works with the others to keep the plant or animal alive. Some things, such as bacteria, are just one cell; this contains all they need to survive.

THROUGH THE WALLS

Each animal cell is surrounded by a thin membrane. This gives it shape and lets chemicals and waste pass in and out. Inside the membrane, tiny structures float in cytoplasm, a jellylike fluid.

INSIDE THE CHAMBER

Each tiny structure, or organelle, in a cell has a job. The nucleus, for example, contains genes (instructions that decide the cell's shape and function). Sausage-shaped structures called mitochondria release the energy in food. Other organelles store energy, make proteins, keep the cell clear of debris, or defend it against bacteria.

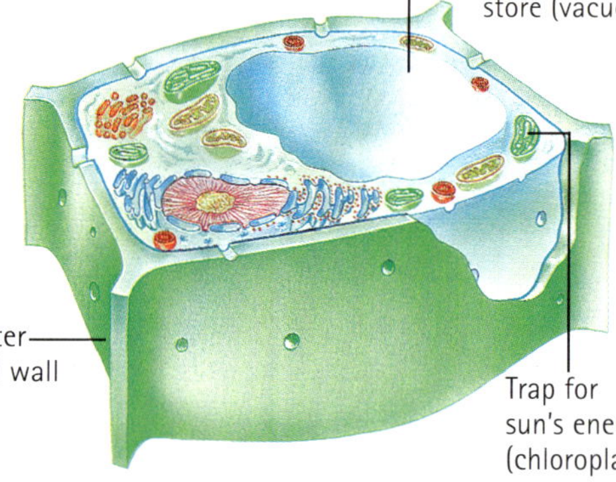

▲ Plant cells have a thick wall of cellulose, which gives them a rigid shape. Up to 90 percent of their space is taken up by the vacuole—a sack full of sugary water.

PLANT CELLS

Unlike animal cells, plant cells have a thick cell wall and extra structures called chloroplasts. These structures are filled with a green pigment called chlorophyll. This traps the sun's energy and uses it to make food in a process called photosynthesis.

SPLITTING IN TWO

Cells multiply by splitting in two. Under a microscope, you can see some bacteria split as fast as once every 15 minutes. Most animal and plant cells multiply much more slowly than this for growth, to repair damage, and for reproduction.

ANIMAL CELLS

Every part of an animal—from its bones to its blood—is made of cells. Many of the cells are spherical, but unevenly shaped, because they do not have a thick outer wall like plant cells. They all have the same basic structures inside them, known as organelles.

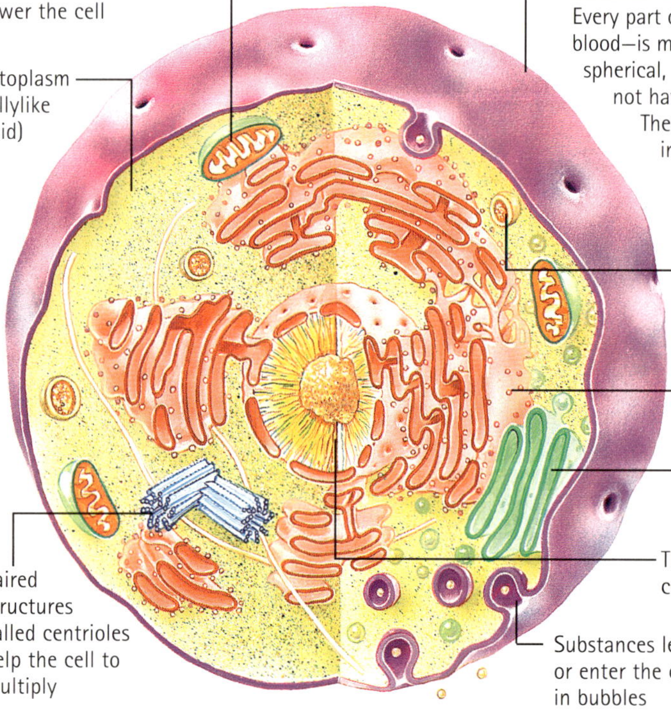

SEE ALSO
Brain and nervous system, Disease, Genetics, Reproduction

Celt

The Celts are a group of people who lived in Europe from about 2,500 years ago. They were fierce warriors who fought frequently.

This Celtic silver and gold drinking cup was made in Ireland in the A.D. 700s.

A Celtic noble or priest would have worn this gold torque around his neck.

A brooch, from the 500s, used to fasten a woolen cloak around the shoulders.

The first Celts lived in central Europe from about 500 B.C. and came to live in countries such as Germany, France, Britain, and Spain. Most of what we know about Celtic life and culture has been passed down in accounts written by the Romans.

FARMING AND METALWORK

The Celts lived by farming the land, growing grain, root crops, and fruit, and breeding cattle, sheep, and pigs. They were skilled metalworkers, famous for gold jewelry. During the Iron Age, they made high-quality weapons and armor.

TRIBAL WARS

Celtic tribes fought fierce battles with their rivals. Warriors wore little armor, sometimes fighting naked to prove their bravery. Many tribes built fortifications on hills for protection. In Britain, Queen Boudicca (or Boadicea) led her tribe, the Iceni, in a failed attack on the Romans in A.D. 61.

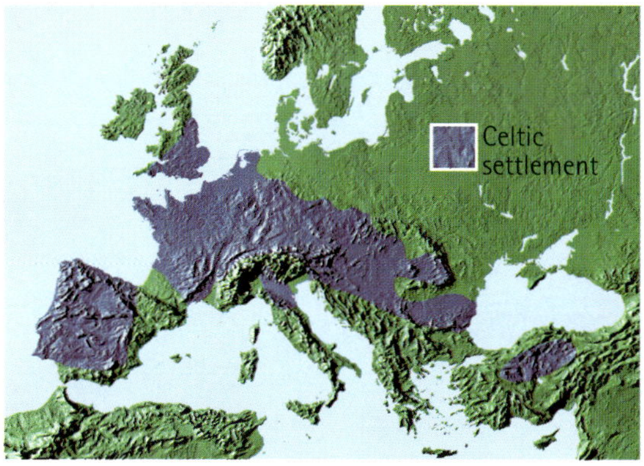

▲ This map shows the major areas of Celtic settlement in about 200 B.C. Celtic people living in Turkey were called Galatians, while in France they were called Gauls.

GODS AND DRUIDS

The Celts had no written language, but passed on stories of their gods and history in songs and poems. They worshiped many different gods and goddesses, offering sacrifices in their honor. Ceremonies and rituals were performed by Druidic priests.

TODAY'S CELTS

Most Celtic tribes were conquered by about A.D. 150, during the spread of the Roman Empire. Today, Celtic people can be found in the British Isles and in Brittany, in France.

WARRIOR QUEEN

Queen Maeve ruled Celtic Connaught in Ireland in about A.D. 100. According to a later legendary story, "The Cattle Raid of Cooley," she attacked Ulster in order to capture a brown bull to complete her collection of prized items. She captured the animal, but was later defeated by another Celt, Cuchulainn.

SEE ALSO

France, Ireland (Republic of), Roman Empire

CENTRAL AMERICA

Central America is a strip of land between North and South America. It consists of Belize, Guatemala, Costa Rica, El Salvador, Honduras, Nicaragua, and Panama.

BELIZE
Area: 8,866 sq. mi.
Population: 224,663
Capital: Belmopan
Languages: English and Spanish
Currency: Belize dollar

COSTA RICA
Area: 19,238 sq. mi.
Population: 3,534,174
Capital: San José
Language: Spanish
Currency: Colón

EL SALVADOR
Area: 8,236 sq. mi.
Population: 5,661,827
Capital: San Salvador
Language: Spanish
Currency: Colón

GUATEMALA
Area: 42,042 sq. mi.
Population: 11,558,407
Capital: Guatemala City
Language: Spanish
Currency: Quetzal

Poverty, political instability, and civil war have troubled Central America for the last 100 years. All seven countries in this region are rich in natural resources, but wealth is spread unevenly. A growing number of people earn money from tourism, but 40 percent still work on the land, earning barely enough to survive.

LAND AND CLIMATE

Lowland forests, plains, and swamps lie along the Central American coasts, and rivers and mountains crisscross the region. Its many volcanoes include Guatemala's Tajumulco, the highest peak in Central America. The region's climate is hot and moist, with temperatures seldom dropping below 75°F (24°C). Land along the coast has the highest temperatures, with cooler areas inland on the mountains and plateaus (flat areas of land high above sea level). More than 12 in. (300mm) of rain per month falls in some areas from July to September.

FORESTS IN DANGER

Central America has some of the richest forests in the world, containing valuable hardwood trees, such as mahogany. But in some places, including Costa Rica, the trees are being cut down so fast for timber, or to make space for farming, that national parks have been set up to protect the remaining trees. Jaguars, monkeys, snakes, caimans (like small alligators), iguanas, many species of bird, as well as colorful butterflies and other insects are all at risk from deforestation.

▲ The Mayan temple of Altun Ha lies deep in the rain forest of Belize. Hundreds of palaces and pyramids were built by the Maya in Central America between A.D. 300 and A.D. 900.

AGRICULTURAL LIFE

The majority of people in Central America are farmers. Cattle and sheep are raised in upland areas; export crops, such as bananas, sugarcane, cotton, and about one tenth of the world's coffee supply, are grown on plantations. Chicle (for chewing gum) is collected from sapodilla trees, and cacao beans are farmed for chocolate. Indian corn, beans, and rice are grown for food.

▼ Most Central Americans are Roman Catholic, but their religious festivals often have a local flavor. For example, All Saints' Day (November 1) is celebrated in Guatemala with riotous horse races.

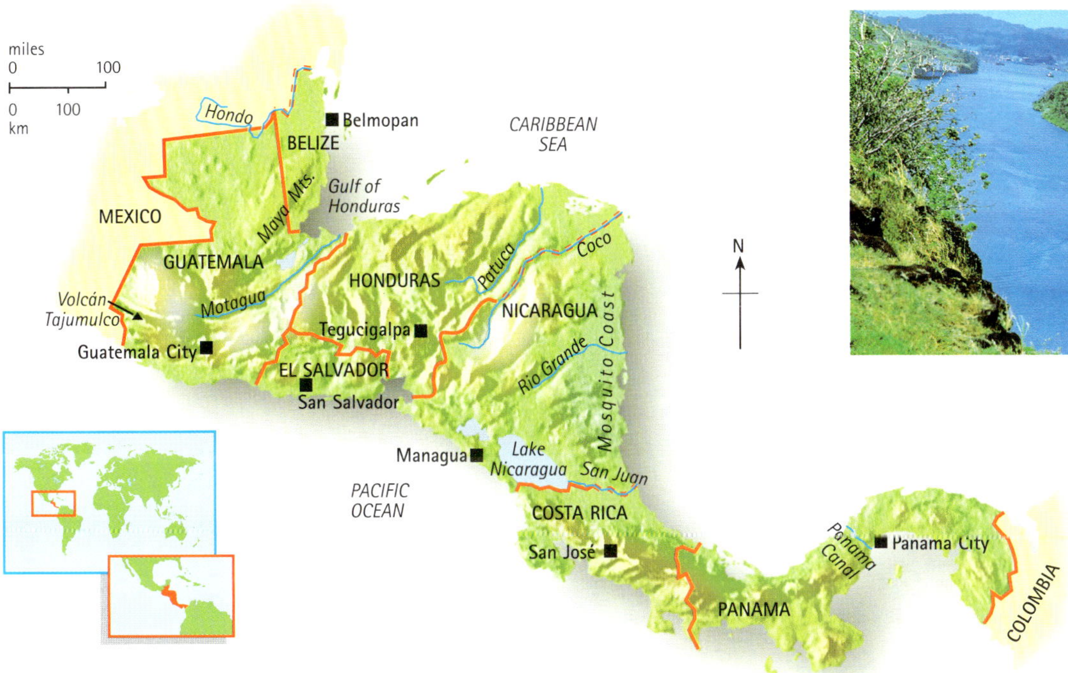

◀ There are many Indian communities in Guatemala, each with its own distinct style of dress.

HONDURAS
Area: 59,160 sq. mi.
Population: 5,751,384
Capital: Tegucigalpa
Language: Spanish
Currency: Lempira

NICARAGUA
Area: 57,143 sq. mi.
Population: 4,386,399
Capital: Managua
Languages: Spanish and English
Currency: Córdoba

PANAMA
Area: 29,129 sq. mi.
Population: 2,693,417
Capital: Panama City
Languages: Spanish and English
Currency: Balboa

INDUSTRIAL GROWTH

Migration to the cities in Central America is growing, but jobs are scarce since industry is still limited to small factories making clothing, household items, and shoes. Handmade pottery, woolen rugs, leatherwork, and hats are sold to tourists.

PEOPLE AND LANGUAGE

Most Central Americans are of mixed European and Indian descent. In the 1500s, Spanish soldiers and gold seekers conquered the region. Before then, it was home to various Indian tribes, including the Maya who ruled between A.D. 300 and A.D. 900. Many of the first European settlers brought African slaves, whose descendants still live in Belize, Nicaragua, and Panama. Spanish is spoken all over the region, although English is the official language in Belize. Many people also speak local Indian languages.

INDEPENDENT NATIONS

Honduras, Guatemala, El Salvador, Costa Rica, and Nicaragua gained independence from Spain in the 1800s. Panama separated from Colombia in 1903, and Belize was a British colony until 1981. In the 1960s, the Central American Common Market was set up to create unity between all the countries, but until recently, civil war and political instability have made this difficult. Today, renewed efforts are being made for greater cooperation between members.

◀ Many Guatemalan village women weave traditional textiles to sell to tourists.

SEE ALSO
Aztec, Civil war, Conservation, Maya

CHEMISTRY

Chemistry is the study of chemicals. These are substances that are used in, or created by, a reaction involving changes to atoms or molecules.

ANTOINE LAVOISIER (1743–94). Lavoisier was a French chemist. He explained how chemical reactions worked. He was the first to understand the role of oxygen in combustion (burning).

CHEMICAL ANALYSIS

Chemists use flame tests as a way of identifying chemical elements—by seeing which color they give off when held in the flame of a Bunsen burner. A compound of an element is burned on the end of a piece of platinum wire or asbestos. The flame burns a distinctive color and so the element can be identified. This type of chemical analysis is called qualitative, and shows what elements a substance contains. To show how much of an element is present, chemists use quantitative analysis.

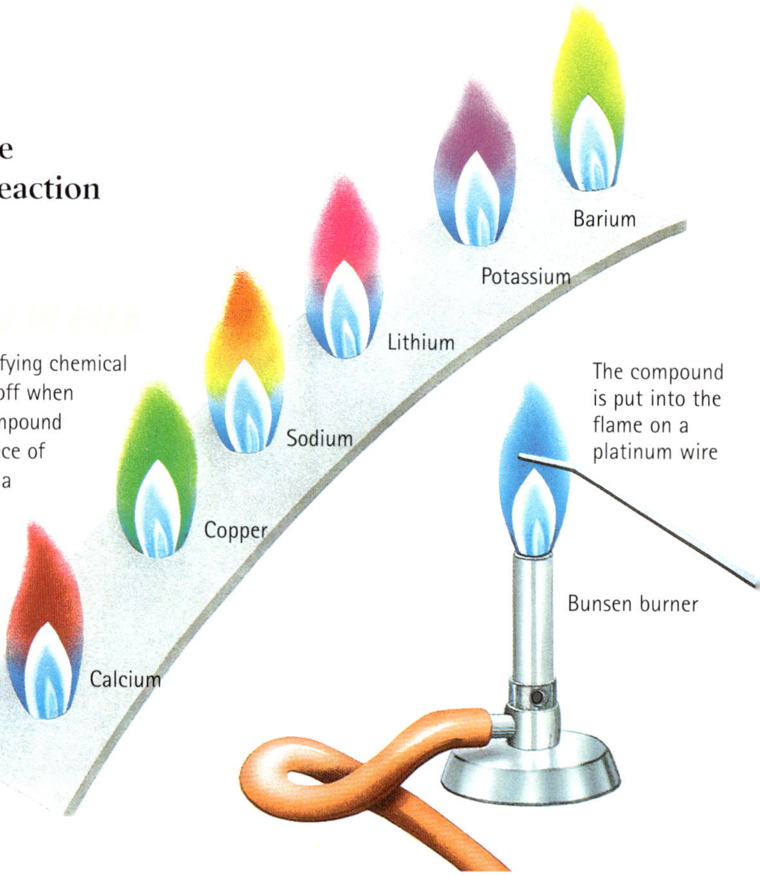

Flame colors of elements

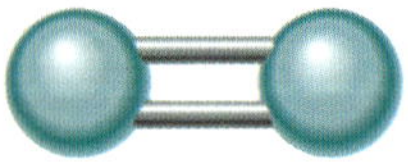

Oxygen is an element. The two atoms that make up its molecules are of the same kind. The chemical formula for oxygen is O_2.

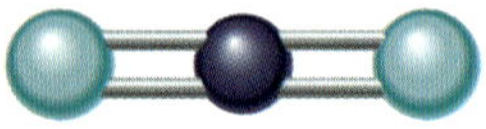

Carbon dioxide gas is a compound of two oxygen atoms with one carbon atom. Its chemical formula is written CO_2.

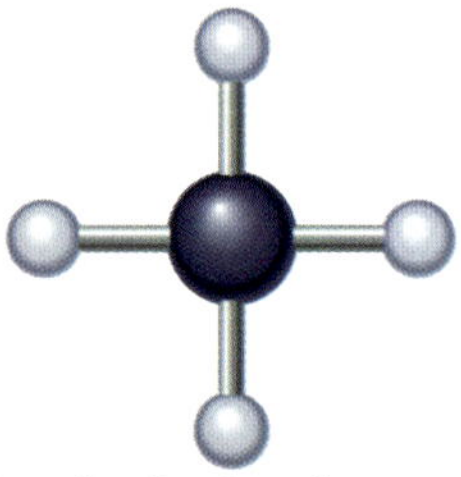

A molecule of methane gas has a carbon atom in the middle bonded to four hydrogen atoms. Its formula is written CH_4.

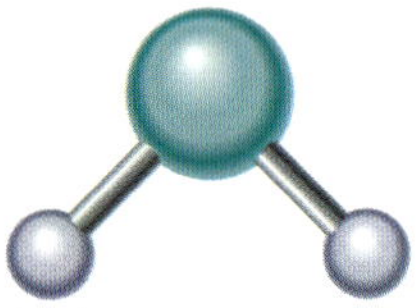

Water has one oxygen atom and two hydrogen atoms, giving it probably the best-known chemical formula, H_2O.

Chemistry explains the way substances behave and how they combine with each other. Chemists use chemical reactions to create many substances used in everyday life, including plastics, dyes, glues, detergents, and medicines.

ELEMENTS AND COMPOUNDS

An element is a substance in which all the atoms are of the same kind. A compound is a combination of two or more elements. The compound sodium chloride (common salt), for example, is a combination of the elements sodium and chlorine. Many compounds, including salt and water, occur naturally. Others, such as nylon and plastic, were first made artificially in laboratories.

CHEMICAL REACTIONS

When different substances combine to form new materials, a chemical reaction has taken place. A substance's atoms are bonded together into molecules. During a reaction, the bonds between atoms break, allowing new molecules to form. A rusting car is an example of a chemical reaction, as iron in the car and oxygen in the air form iron oxide, or rust. Chemists use symbols (such as Fe for iron and O for oxygen) to record what happens in a reaction.

ALCHEMISTS TO SCIENTISTS

Medieval alchemists studied reactions, but it was not until the 1770s that Antoine Lavoisier showed how reactions work. In 1869, Russian chemist Dmitri Mendeleyev worked out the periodic table, grouping elements by how they react with each other.

WEAPONS AND DRUGS

Today, chemical substances of all kinds are mined or manufactured. Chemists search for new reactions to create fertilizers or drugs, which may contain long chains of molecules. Industry mass-produces useful chemicals through large-scale reactions. Poison gas and other chemicals have been used as weapons, but they are now banned.

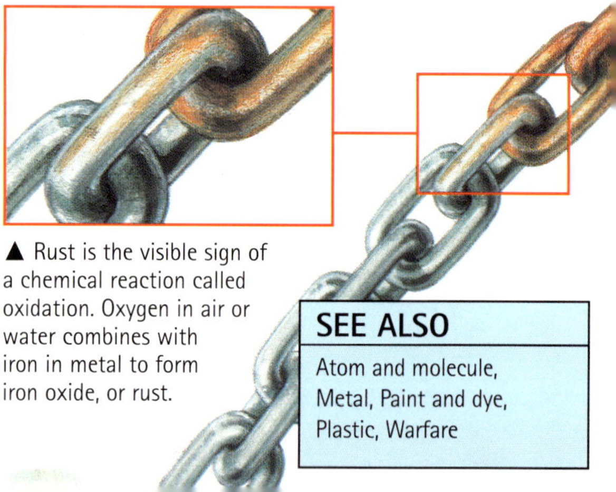

▲ Rust is the visible sign of a chemical reaction called oxidation. Oxygen in air or water combines with iron in metal to form iron oxide, or rust.

SEE ALSO

Atom and molecule, Metal, Paint and dye, Plastic, Warfare

CHINA

China is the third largest country in the world and the nation with the largest population. Almost a fourth of the Earth's people live in China.

Area: 3,691,502 sq. mi.
Population: 1,179,470,000
Capital: Beijing
Language: Mandarin
Currency: Yuan

China is one of the world's oldest civilizations. Its name comes from an ancient Chinese ruling family called Qin (pronounced Ch'in). The Chinese call their country Zhongguo, which means "middle land." China's 1.2 billion citizens are ruled by one of the world's few remaining communist governments.

NATURAL BARRIERS

China lies in eastern Asia; deserts and mountains form natural barriers with its neighbors. The Gobi Desert—502,000 sq. mi. (1,300,000sq km)—straddles the border with Mongolia. The Himalayas—the highest mountains on Earth, rising to almost 5 mi. (8,000m)—stretch along the border with India, Bhutan, and Nepal. The Chang (Yangtze) River is the longest in Asia and flows from the Tibetan uplands to the East China Sea, dividing the warm, moist southern regions from the drier and cooler north.

▲ The bicycle is China's main method of transportation. More than 17 million bicycles are made there each year.

▲ The giant panda lives in the bamboo forests of central and western China. So few now survive in the wild that it has become a worldwide symbol for conservation.

CHINA'S WILDLIFE

Plant life ranges from bamboos and other subtropical plants in the south to coniferous forests in the north. Garden plants now common around the world, such as wisteria, first came from China. With much of the country covered by mountains and desert, forests have been cleared to make way for villages and farms. This has reduced the habitats of animals such as the tiger (which is also prey to hunters) and the giant panda, making them rare in the wild. ▶

THE GREAT WALL OF CHINA

One of China's greatest early empires was ruled by the Qin dynasty. The first Qin emperor, Shi Huangdi, came to the throne in 221 B.C. He ordered the construction of the Great Wall to keep out invaders from the north. Stretching for 4,000 mi. (6,400km), the wall was built by joining together shorter walls that had been built earlier. The wall has been rebuilt many times. Most of the present wall was constructed during the Ming Dynasty (1368–1644).

A NATION OF FARMERS

About 70 percent of people farm the land. Many farms are run as collectives, with people working together and dividing crops between the government and themselves. Important crops include rice, which is the main food of the south, and wheat, which is used to make bread and noodles in the north. Millet, tea, vegetables, soybeans, and cotton are also grown; and many farmers breed pigs, ducks, and chickens.

▼ Traditional ways of life are still strong in many parts of China. Here, fishermen use birds called cormorants to bring up fish from the water. They tie a thong around the bird's throat to stop it swallowing the catch.

INDUSTRIAL GROWTH

Chinese industry has grown rapidly in the last 40 years. Factories produce machinery, transportation equipment, clothing, and electrical goods. Shanghai is the leading industrial city. In 1997, Hong Kong—then a British colony and wealthy financial and industrial center—was returned to China.

WRITING IN CHARACTERS

Over 90 percent of the people are Han Chinese, originally from the north of China. Mandarin is the main dialect, but many others are also spoken. Chinese writing does not use an alphabet. Instead, it uses symbols called characters that stand for words or ideas, not letters.

PHILOSOPHY AND FAMILY

For more than 2,000 years, Confucianism has been China's main religion. It teaches respect for parents and ancestors and has strongly influenced family life in China. At one time, several generations of the same family lived in the same house. Today, in an effort to curb China's population growth, the government rewards one-child families with priority housing and medical care. This has led to much smaller families.

RULED BY DYNASTIES

For thousands of years, China was an empire ruled by emperors from successive royal families called dynasties. Many great inventions were made by the Chinese, including paper, ink, silk, printing, and gunpowder. China remained isolated from most of the rest of the world until the 1800s, when foreign powers forced China to open its borders to trade. In 1911, dynastic rule was ended and the country became a republic.

COMMUNIST RULE

In 1949, China adopted a communist government and was renamed the People's Republic of China, under the leadership of Mao Tse-tung. His strict policies meant that there were many changes as all aspects of life came under state control, and people found their freedom restricted.

▲ Preparing food on a street stall. Rice, noodles, and vegetables are the main ingredients used in Chinese cooking.

◀ Shanghai is China's largest city, with a population of 13,400,000. It is also China's leading industrial center.

CHINA TODAY

Since Mao's death in 1976, China's government has encouraged economic reform and trade with foreign countries. More and more people are moving from the countryside to cities, attracted by factory jobs and higher standards of living. But political change is limited. In 1989, up to 1,000 protesting students were killed in Beijing's Tiananmen Square.

▶ This man is performing a traditional form of exercise that develops both mind and body. Called wushu, it is an ancient Chinese martial art.

◀ Farmers bring their produce to sell at a market in southern China. Here, farmers harvest three crops a year—two of rice and one of vegetables.

SEE ALSO

Asia, Communism, Mongol Empire, Paper, Zoology

CHRISTIANITY

Christianity is a religion based on the teachings of Jesus Christ, who lived in Palestine about 2,000 years ago. Today, it is practiced throughout the world.

The most well-known symbol of Christianity is the cross. It represents the cross on which Jesus was crucified.

Greek Christians used the fish as a code. The Greek word for fish spelled out the first letters of "Jesus Christ, God's Son, Savior."

The Christian Bible consists of the Hebrew Bible (Old Testament) and Christ's life and teachings (New Testament).

More people follow the Christian religion than any other. About 1.5 billion people believe that there is only one God and that he sent his son to Earth to save people from sin.

THE LIFE OF CHRIST

The life and teachings of Jesus Christ are contained in the New Testament of the Bible, the Christians' holy book. (The Old Testament of the Bible contains the sacred writings of the Jews.) Jesus is said to have performed miracles and healed the sick. The Roman rulers of Jerusalem crucified him by nailing him to a cross. Christians believe that three days later Jesus was raised from the dead, and that some 40 days later he rose into Heaven.

CHRISTIANITY SPREADS

Jesus' teachings were spread by his disciples, or followers, who formed the early church. Despite persecution, Christianity became the religion of the Roman Empire in A.D. 324 and later spread across the world. Today, there are three main divisions in the Christian Church: Roman Catholic, Protestant, and

▲ Upon entering the Christian faith, followers are baptized, or dipped in water. This symbolizes cleansing and reflects the way Jesus was baptized by John the Baptist.

Eastern Orthodox. About one billion people are Catholics.

THREE-IN-ONE GOD

Christians believe that God is a Trinity: the Father (God), the Son (Jesus), and the Holy Spirit (God's influence on Earth).

THE HOLY MEAL

Before his Crucifixion, Jesus ate the Last Supper with his disciples. Christians reenact this meal with bread and wine in a special church ceremony called Holy Communion, or Mass, when Christ "becomes present" again. They celebrate Christ's birth at Christmas and his Resurrection at Easter, and the coming of the Holy Spirit at Pentecost.

▲ On Palm Sunday (the Sunday before Easter), many Christians carry palms in church. This commemorates Jesus' entry into Jerusalem, when he was greeted with branches of palm.

► The leader of the Roman Catholic Church is the Pope. Catholics believe he is God's representative on Earth.

SEE ALSO

Crusades, Religion, Renaissance, Roman Empire

CITY

A city is a large community where thousands of people live and work. Nearly half of the world's population lives in cities.

Most cities are commercial or administrative centers. They are usually larger and more important than other towns in their region. Not all cities are huge. In Europe, a city is a town with a cathedral. In the United States, "city" is applied to an urban area with definite boundaries. The world's largest city is Tokyo in Japan, with over 25 million people, including those living in suburbs.

FAST FACTS

- The five largest cities in order of size are: Tokyo (Japan), São Paulo (Brazil), New York (U.S.A.), Mexico City (Mexico), and Shanghai (China)
- One hundred years ago, London was the largest city in the world
- By the 100s B.C., Rome was the first city to have a population of more than one million
- Vatican City in Rome is the world's smallest state

CITY LOCATIONS

The earliest cities grew in areas where the climate was suitable for growing crops. Access was also important so that trade could develop. Venice in Italy, London in England, and Calcutta in India all grew because of their closeness to water, which provided transportation routes.

PLANNING AHEAD

Most of today's cities were not planned, but spread out as they grew. In 1692, William Penn, the founder of the state of Pennsylvania, drew a plan for Philadelphia that resembled a grid. This became the pattern for most U.S. cities. In the mid-1800s, a French administrator called Baron Georges-Eugene Haussmann redesigned Paris with wide boulevards and open squares rather than the chaotic maze of small streets that the city had been before.

CAPITAL CITIES

Every country has a capital city where the national government is located. During the 1900s, a few capital cities were designed and built from new, including Canberra in Australia, Brasília in Brazil, and Islamabad in Pakistan. But more often, capitals have grown over time and have a mixture of old and new buildings alongside each other. The oldest parts of a city often form the center. Many people live outside the city center in areas known as suburbs.

HOW CITIES WORK

With city centers becoming busier and more densely packed, high-rise buildings make the most of limited space. People working in the city often move farther out, where land is cheaper. This means that good road and train systems are necessary to bring them into the center.

▲ Large, elegant department stores attract tourists and shoppers to cities.

▲ The opera and other forms of entertainment bring people to the city center. They are often performed in grand and ornate buildings.

▲ Placing mass transit systems underground creates more space in cities.

▲ A good road network and public transportation are important to link the city with the suburbs.

SEE ALSO

Housing, Road, Skyscraper, Train, Transportation

CIVIL RIGHTS

Civil rights are the laws and customs that entitle everyone to fair and equal treatment. They give people the freedom to speak and act within the law.

AMNESTY INTERNATIONAL
AMNISTÍA INTERNACIONAL
AMNISTIE INTERNATIONALE
МЕЖДУНАРОДНАЯ АМНИСТИЯ
منظمة العفو الدولية
國際特赦組織

▲ Amnesty International works for the freeing of political prisoners and prisoners of conscience. It campaigns against torture and the death penalty.

▲ The flag of the United Nations, which was set up in 1946, after the end of World War II. The aim of the UN is to maintain international peace and cooperation.

The idea of civil rights in the West dates back to the writings of Ancient Greek and Roman philosophers, and to the ideas of Judaism and Christianity. In some countries, civil rights are protected by a written constitution, as in the United States; in others, such as the United Kingdom, they consist of laws and customs built up over hundreds of years.

FAIR AND EQUAL

Civil rights mean people must be treated fairly and equally, no matter what their sex, religion, or ethnic origin. They are allowed freedom to express what they believe in speech or in the media. They also have the right to organize a political party, to have a fair trial if accused of a crime, and to vote in elections.

THE FIGHT FOR THE RIGHT

Many rights have been won only after a long and painful struggle. During the 1950s and 1960s, Dr. Martin Luther King led the civil rights campaign to win equality for black Americans. In South Africa, Nelson Mandela was imprisoned in 1962 for opposing apartheid (the separation of whites and nonwhites). He was finally released in 1991, when apartheid was abolished. In 1994, Mandela was elected South Africa's first black president.

▲ A demonstration held in 1997 against the military government in Myanmar (Burma). The government had refused to recognize the results of recent elections.

CIVIL RIGHTS ABUSES

International bodies, such as the United Nations and the European Court of Human Rights, protect civil rights; other organizations, like Amnesty International, campaign on behalf of people who are persecuted. However, some governments continue to ban civil rights. Dictators and single-party states deny rights to their people because they do not want their power threatened. Communist countries, such as China, traditionally stress the importance of social rights—for example, the right to work—often at the expense of human rights like freedom of speech.

"I HAVE A DREAM"

In 1963, Martin Luther King led 200,000 people on a civil rights march in Washington, D.C. In his speech he declared, "I have a dream," demanding equal rights for black Americans. The Civil Rights Act of 1964 followed, and King was awarded the Nobel Peace Prize. In 1968 he was shot.

SEE ALSO
Communism, Democracy, Fascism, South Africa

Civil war

Civil war is an armed struggle between people who live in the same country or nation. Civil war is usually triggered by political, religious, or ethnic differences.

▲ An Angolan UNITA rebel soldier pictured in 1986. Angola has suffered years of civil war, backed, until 1990, by countries such as Cuba, the Soviet Union, South Africa, and the United States.

Families, communities, and whole countries have been divided by civil war. Because fighting takes place wholly within a country, no one escapes its effects. Prisoners are often murdered, homes destroyed, and civilians terrorized.

FIGHTING FOR RIGHTS

Civil wars erupt because of a difference in people's beliefs. They are often begun by minorities fighting for greater political or religious rights, for union with a similar group in a nearby state, or for the right to keep their way of life. These minorities are often led by strong figures.

OUTSIDE INFLUENCE

In some civil wars, outside countries give their support to one side, often for political gain or to protect human rights. During the 1980s, for example, a desperate civil war raged in Nicaragua between the socialist government and the right-wing Contras. The U.S.A. supported the Contras in order to combat the spread of left-wing socialist and communist regimes in Central America. Such foreign interference was typical of the Cold War, a period of rivalry and deep distrust between the Soviet Union, the U.S.A., and their supporters.

▲ A United Nations soldier helps an old woman cross the main street in Sarajevo, in the former Yugoslavia. An armored vehicle shields them from sniper fire.

KEY DATES

1918–21 Russian Civil War. Fought between Bolsheviks and anti-Communists. Bolsheviks win

1967–70 Nigerian Civil War. Fought between Biafra and the Federal government. Biafra is defeated

1968– Civil war in Northern Ireland. Prolonged conflict between Protestants and Catholics. A cease-fire is called and peace talks begin in 1994

1971 Pakistan Civil War. Fought between Bangladesh (east Pakistan) and west Pakistan. Bangladesh wins

ETHNIC CLASHES

Civil wars started by ethnic (racial) hatred have produced some of the worst cruelties of recent times. In the early 1990s, fighting broke out in Yugoslavia, as three provinces—Bosnia, Croatia, and Slovenia—fought for independence from the Serbian-dominated state. During the long-running war, thousands of civilians became the innocent victims of ethnic cleansing—the murder or forced eviction of one racial group by another through the use of violence and terror.

AFRICAN UNREST

When colonial rule ended in many African nations in the 1960s and 1970s, civil war followed. Within countries like Nigeria and Angola, different peoples had been forced together by colonial boundaries and these differences caused conflict. Some of the bloodiest civil wars caused by political and ethnic differences have broken out in Somalia, Congo, and Chad.

► A guerrilla fighter in Afghanistan. During the 1980s, Afghans fought to free their country from Soviet control. Guerrillas carried out surprise attacks on depots and patrols.

▲ Posters are often used to rally support. This poster declares, "Peasants, the land is yours." It was designed by Republicans in the Spanish Civil War.

▼ Spanish army soldiers forcing Republicans to surrender at Sanosierra on August 6, 1936.

CHARLES I
English ruler (1600–49), came to the throne in 1625. His execution ended the English Civil War.

OLIVER CROMWELL
(1599–1658) ruled England, Scotland, and Ireland as Lord Protector after the king's execution.

ROMAN CIVIL WAR

Civil wars are not a new phenomenon. Many of the earliest civil wars were fought between influential individuals and their backers in the search for power. In 49 B.C., civil war was started in Rome when Julius Caesar ordered his armies to cross the Rubicon River and march on Rome. He drove out his opponents and succeeded in making himself dictator.

ENGLISH CIVIL WAR

The English Civil War, which lasted from 1642 to 1649, was a struggle between the English king, Charles I, and parliament over who should govern the country. Charles believed that kings were appointed by God and should rule alone. Parliament believed it should have greater power. Parliament refused to cooperate with the king and this caused civil war.

ROYALISTS AND ROUNDHEADS

England divided into two factions: the Royalists, or Cavaliers, supported the king; the Roundheads supported Parliament. Two great generals, Lord Fairfax and Oliver Cromwell, led the Roundheads, and eventually the king's forces were defeated. In 1649, Charles was executed and England was declared a republic.

THE SPANISH CIVIL WAR

In 1936, a left-wing Republican government was elected in Spain. Most of the right-wing army rebelled and tried to overthrow the government. France and the Soviet Union backed the Republicans. The right, led by General Franco, received support from Germany and Italy. Thousands of Spaniards died in the war. In 1939, the Republican army collapsed and Franco became dictator of Spain.

► The Roundheads' crushing defeat of Royalist forces at Naseby in 1645 was the decisive victory of the English Civil War.

SEE ALSO
Africa, Civil War (American) Greece and the Balkans, Refugee, Spain and Portugal, Warfare

CIVIL WAR, AMERICAN

More Americans died in the Civil War than in any other conflict. It was caused by the deep divisions between northern and southern states.

The Union flag (above) and the Confederate flag (left)

The American Civil War (1861–65) was caused by deep political differences. The southern states believed in the right of states, not Congress, to make their own laws, including the right to hold slaves. The South felt that this right was threatened by the election of Abraham Lincoln in 1860.

NORTH AND SOUTH

The North was a land of industry and manufacturing—and home to a strong movement against slavery. The South was a land of farms and plantations and depended on slaves for labor.

A Union soldier

A Confederate soldier

DECLARATION OF WAR

After Lincoln's election, 11 southern states seceded (separated) from the Union to create the Confederate States of America. Southern forces attacked Fort Sumter on April 12, 1861. Lincoln, determined to keep the nation intact, formed the Union army against the slaveholding states.

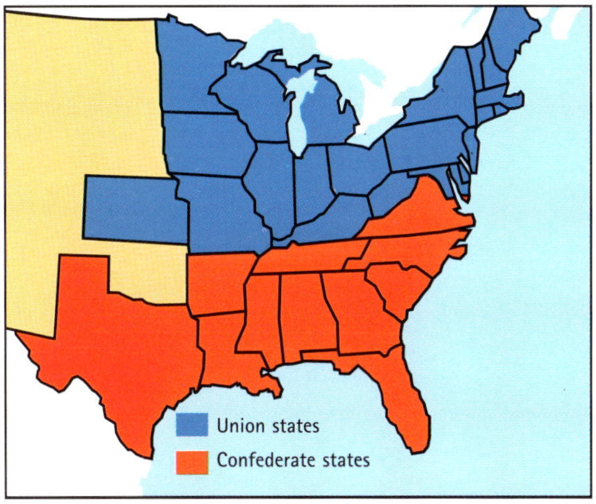

▲ The American Civil War was fought mainly in the East and Southeast between the southern, or Confederate states, and the northern, or Union states, including Oregon and California on the West Coast.

FOUR YEARS OF FIGHTING

The American Civil War was a fight the South could not win. More people lived in the North, it had a stronger industrial base, better communications, and a navy capable of stopping food and supplies reaching the South. In 1865, the South surrendered. More than 600,000 had died in the struggle, and most southern cities had been destroyed by the war. That same year, the 13th Amendment was added to the Constitution, abolishing slavery. Five days after the South's surrender, Lincoln was assassinated.

THE BATTLE OF GETTYSBURG

The Battle of Gettysburg in July 1863 was a major turning point in the American Civil War. About 85,000 Union troops, led by General George Meade, defeated some 75,000 Confederate soldiers led by General Robert E. Lee. The Confederates never truly recovered from the crushing defeat.

SEE ALSO

Slavery, United States of America, Warfare

CLIMATE

The climate of a region is its weather pattern over a long period of time. The weather may change from day to day, but the climate stays the same.

▼ The world can be divided into different climate zones. These vary from tropical regions, characterized by hot and humid weather, to freezing polar areas.

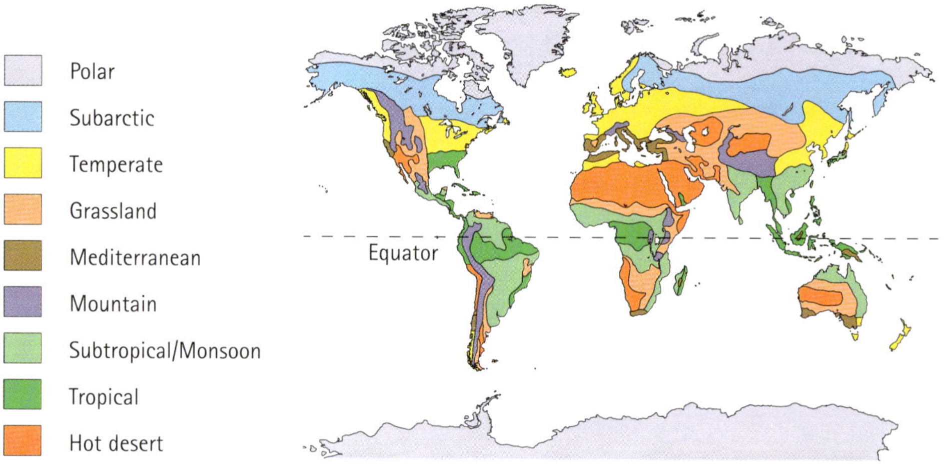

▲ At the equator, the sun's rays are direct and strong. Away from the equator, the sun's rays are weaker because they strike the Earth at an angle and must travel farther through the cool air of the atmosphere.

The climate of a region depends on how close the region is to the sea, how high up it is (its altitude), and, most importantly, how far it is from the equator (its latitude). Climate is usually measured as a combination of the average rainfall in an area and the temperature.

THE POWER OF THE SUN

The two extremes of climate on Earth are found at the equator and at the Poles. The climate is hottest in the zones on either side of the equator—the tropics—because the sun is almost directly overhead. The Poles are the coldest areas: temperatures drop below –58°F (–50°C).

THE TROPICS

The tropics are not only the hottest areas but also the wettest. The intense heat evaporates water from the rivers and oceans, forming rain clouds that drench the tropics. By the time the wet tropical air reaches deserts like the Sahara, in Africa, however, just the other side of the rain forests, it has lost most of its moisture.

COLDER HIGHER UP

Air is cooler the higher you go in the atmosphere. So mountainous regions have a colder climate than low areas. On a mountain, air cools by 42.8°F (6°C) for each 3,300 ft. (1,000m) climbed.

CHANGING CLIMATE

Climates can change over time. Volcanic eruptions may have a sudden, local effect, but deforestation and destruction of the ozone layer by pollutant gases may have long-term effects all over the world.

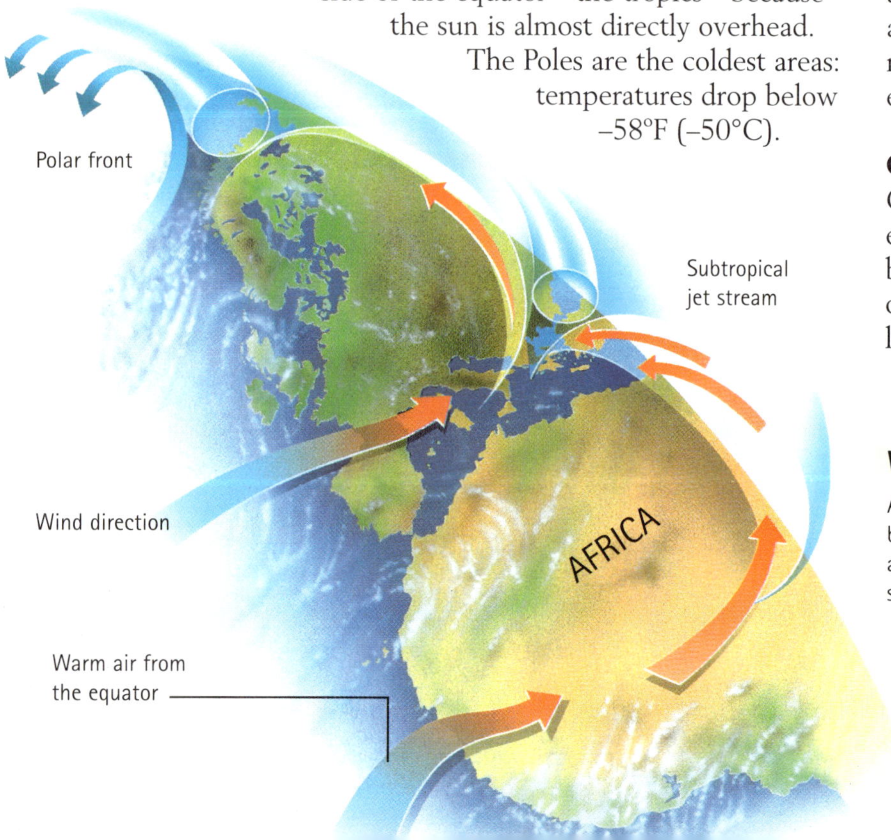

WIND CIRCULATION

At the Poles, cold air sinks and disperses and is replaced by warmer air flowing in from above. The cold air moving away from the Poles meets warm winds from the subtropics and pushes the warm air back to the equator.

SEE ALSO
Desert, Forest, Habitat, Mountain and valley, Pollution, Water, Weather

CLOCK

Clocks are instruments used to measure time in hours, minutes, and seconds down to the smallest fraction. They include mechanical, quartz, and atomic clocks.

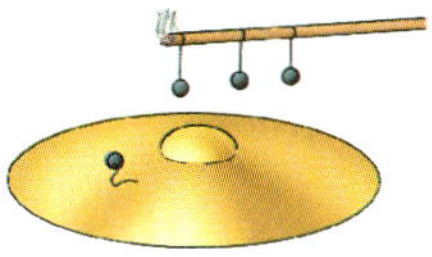

Chinese candle clocks "chime" when the candle burns the string to release a weight onto the cymbal.

Sundials show the time by plotting the changing position of the sun's shadow during the day.

Chronometers, invented in the 1700s for use on ships, have a slowly unwinding spring, not a pendulum.

A quartz watch tells the time by recording the vibrations of a quartz crystal inside.

Atomic clocks count the vibrations of light given off by atoms, and are used in satellites and aircraft.

People first learned to tell the time using sundials, sandglasses, marked candles, and water clocks. But during the 1200s, the first mechanical clocks were made.

MECHANICAL CLOCKS

Mechanical clocks are set in motion in one of two ways—by winding up a spring or by raising a weight. Gearwheels with teeth move the hour, minute, and second hands—this is called the clock's movement. Some clocks need to be wound every day, but others can run for about a week.

THE PENDULUM

In 1582, the Italian scientist Galileo Galilei discovered that every swing of a pendulum, or hanging weight, takes the same length of time. The time the swing takes depends on the length of the pendulum arm. A Dutch astronomer called Christiaan Huygens used this knowledge to make the first pendulum clock 74 years later. In a pendulum clock, the swinging weight moves from side to side to regulate the movements of the clock's hands around the clock face.

QUARTZ CRYSTAL

Most of today's clocks and watches are battery-operated and have a tiny quartz crystal inside. The crystal vibrates when it receives a charge of electricity from the battery. It gives out regular, fast pulses of current, which are slowed down by a microchip to one per second.

ATOMIC CLOCKS

The most accurate clocks are cesium beam atomic clocks, which were first made in 1955. These measure the frequency of an atom's vibrations. They lose only a fraction of a second every million years.

TURNING TIME

When a grandfather clock is wound up, a weight is pulled up to the top of its case. As the weight falls, tiny toothed gearwheels turn and move the hands around the clock face. The swing of the pendulum makes the weight fall evenly as the gears catch against the pallet at every swing, turning one notch of the escape wheel. This makes the "tick-tock" sound.

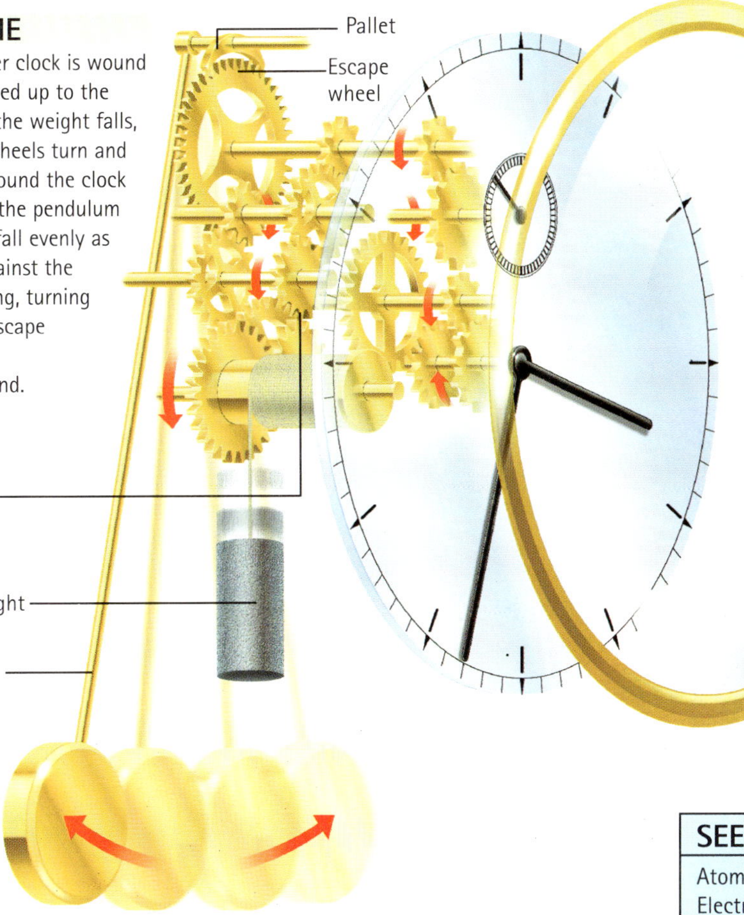

SEE ALSO

Atom and molecule, Electronics, Time

CLOTHING

Clothing is worn to protect the body and to make it look attractive. The kind of clothes people wear reflects where they live, their lifestyle, and their personality.

▲ Firefighters' protective suits were developed from space suit technology. The suits have many layers, which were originally intended to protect astronauts from the sun's lethal radiation while they worked in space.

People started wearing clothes more than 100,000 years ago in colder parts of the world. Ice Age hunters 25,000 years ago stayed warm by sewing animal furs together. About 10,000 years ago, early farming communities learned how to spin plant and animal fibers to make thread that could be woven into cloth. Wool, cotton, silk, and flax for linen were used. Woolen cloth was used in cold northern areas; linen was preferred in hot countries such as Egypt.

THE FIRST PANTS

Among the first people to cut clothes into the kinds of shapes used today were the ancient tribes of Persia (Iran). Men wore coats with sleeves and an early form of pants designed for life on horseback.

READY TO WEAR

In 1785, the steam-powered loom marked the birth of the modern clothing industry; and in the 1850s, sewing machines arrived. Clothing factories soon started making large amounts of inexpensive, ready-to-wear clothes so that people could afford to buy garments instead of making their own or having expensive designs made up by dressmakers and tailors.

CHANGING SHAPES

Advances in technology have continued to shape fashion in the 1900s. Synthetic nylon was first used to make stockings in the 1940s, easy wash-and-wear polyester appeared in the 1960s, and Lycra became fashionable in the 1980s.

▲ In the 1960s, designers responded to a new teenage market, and the miniskirt arrived. Twiggy, shown here, was a British fashion model who became the symbol of the new look.

▲ Simple clothes, in natural fibers, worn in loose flowing styles, kept both women and men cool in Ancient Egypt.

▲ Richly embroidered fabrics were used to make clothes for wealthy people in the 1400s. Men's shoes had long, pointed toes.

▲ Knee breeches in pale colors were worn by gentlemen in the 1700s. Long pants became fashionable during the 1800s.

▲ In the mid-1800s, women wore tight corsets and hoops made of wicker or steel, called crinolines, to make their skirts stick out.

FASHION VICTIMS

Wearing the latest styles to be fashionable began as a way for rich people to show their wealth. But sometimes, staying in fashion was painful. During the 1800s, women in search of the "hourglass" figure wore laced corsets with whalebone inside. This compressed the waist, making it as tiny as possible. People still follow design trends, but since World War II, when many women started working in factories, clothes have become more practical.

WORKWEAR TO CLASSICS

Trends do not always come from designers. Tough denim jeans, originally made as workwear for Californian gold miners in the 1850s, have become fashion classics. Many people today choose clothes to express their personality.

NATIONAL DRESS

In many parts of the world, traditional dress is worn every day. The *sari*, worn by Hindu women, is a long wrap of light fabric worn over a tight-fitting top called a *choli*. In some countries, national dress is kept for festivals and family celebrations.

MIX AND MATCH

National dress has had a strong influence on Western fashion. American cowboys learned to make leather leggings (chaps) by watching Native Americans stretch and soak buffalo hides. Today, designers continue to borrow from different eras and cultures in a constant search for new ideas.

▲ This wet suit is made of neoprene (a synthetic rubber). It gives the diver protection and warmth under water. Clothes like these allow people to explore previously inaccessible places.

▲ Designers' creations are shown on the catwalk, then toned down and reproduced for the ready-to-wear market.

◀ Clothes for sports must be light, protective, and easy to move in. Uniforms often promote a sense of team spirit.

▶ Dressing outrageously is one way to express personality. This person's clothes and hairstyle show that he is a punk.

▲ In the 1800s, young boys and girls from wealthy families dressed alike. Both wore dresses over ankle-length pantaloons.

KEY DATES

1500s Whalebone is first used to stiffen corsets

1850s Tightly laced corsets and crinolines are used to create the "hourglass" figure

1870s The introduction of the bustle in women's dresses

1899 The "Gibson Girl" is created in the U.S.A.

1920s Coco Chanel revolutionizes women's fashion by creating short, simple shift dresses

1947 Christian Dior's "New Look" with very full skirts ends the austerity of the war years

1957 The sack dress dominates U.S. fashion

1960s André Courrèges (France) introduces the miniskirt, which is popularized in the U.K. by Mary Quant

SEE ALSO

Design, France, Material, Paint and dye, Textile

Coal

Coal is a rock formed under the ground from the remains of decayed prehistoric plants. It burns easily and is widely used as a fuel.

Anthracite is the highest quality coal. It gives the most heat but little smoke.

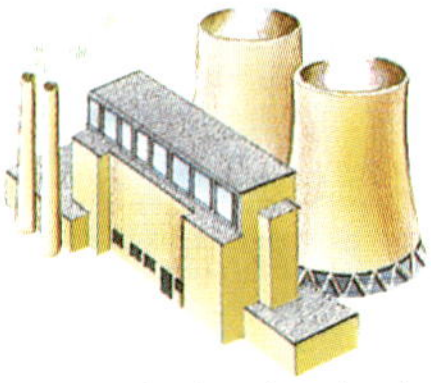

Most coal mined today is used in power plants to produce light and heat.

Some perfumes are made from coal tar—a black liquid produced from coal.

Coal, like petroleum and gas, is a fossil fuel. It was formed under the ground from the remains of plants over millions of years. It is used to make fires and to make electricity, chemicals, and steel.

CARBON CONTENT

Coal is made up of carbon, tar, oils, and minerals. There are three different types of coal, depending on the amount of carbon each contains. Lignite, or brown coal, contains less than 50 percent carbon; bituminous coal around 70 percent; and anthracite, the most valuable, has about 95 percent carbon. Over four billion tons of coal are mined each year and almost 4,000 billion tons remain underground.

INDUSTRIAL COAL

In about 1750, the Industrial Revolution led to a huge demand for coal as a fuel for steam engines. Today, many power plants burn coal to produce electricity. The iron industry uses coke—coal which has been heated to make the tar and oils evaporate—to produce iron and steel. The tar and oils are then used to produce dyes, fertilizers, and fibers such as nylon.

POLLUTION

When coal is burned, it releases smoke containing soot and poisonous gases, such as carbon monoxide. These can harm the environment, so most power plants have filters to clean the smoke.

▲ Different equipment is needed to mine coal. Cutting machines dig out coal within the mine while a conveyor belt transports it back up the shaft.

HOW COAL IS FORMED

About 300 million years ago, in an age known as the Carboniferous period, the climate was warm and wet, ideal for swampy forests. Dead plants rotted and formed peat, which was buried under layers of sand and mud as sea levels rose, flooding the swamps. These layers slowly turned to rock. Their weight squeezed the peat, turning it into coal.

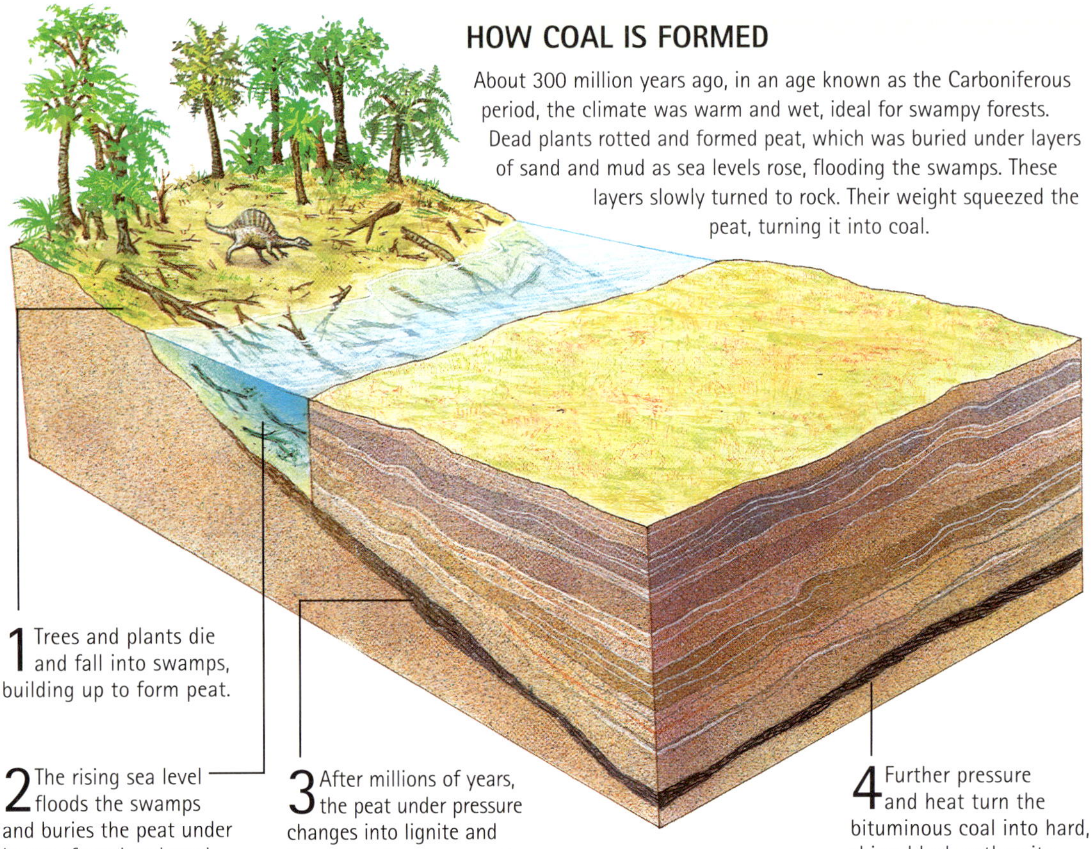

1 Trees and plants die and fall into swamps, building up to form peat.

2 The rising sea level floods the swamps and buries the peat under layers of sand and mud.

3 After millions of years, the peat under pressure changes into lignite and then into bituminous coal.

4 Further pressure and heat turn the bituminous coal into hard, shiny, black anthracite.

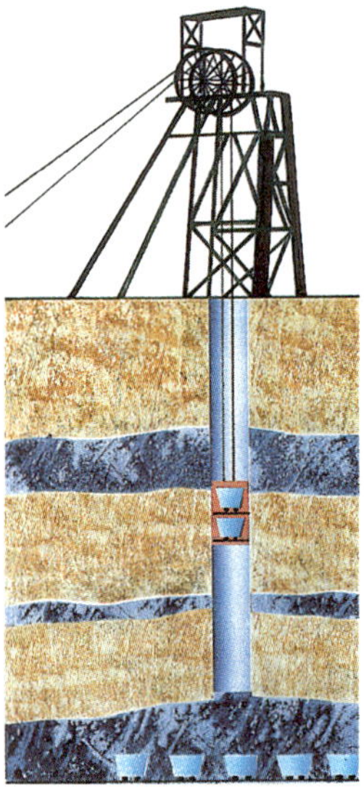

▲ A shaft is dug down to a seam many hundreds of feet below. A few mines are opencast—coal is mined at the surface.

SEE ALSO

Electricity, Fossil, Gas, Industrial Revolution, Iron and steel, Mining, Oil, Pollution

Cold War

The Cold War was a period of hostility between the capitalist and communist countries of the world. It began after the end of World War II.

▲ The U.S.S.R.'s Nikita Khrushchev (left) and U.S. President John F. Kennedy, fingers poised over their nuclear buttons, confront each other in this 1962 cartoon.

FAST FACTS

- In 1955, a Soviet-led alliance of Eastern European states, the Warsaw Pact, was set up to oppose NATO
- In 1945, there were only three nuclear weapons in the world; by 1962, there were over 2,000
- In 1956, an anti-Soviet uprising in Hungary was brutally crushed

For more than 45 years, between 1945 and 1991, two superpowers, the United States and the Soviet Union (U.S.S.R.), fought each other using spies, alliances, trading bans, and local wars as their weapons.

IRON CURTAIN

After World War II, the U.S.S.R. and the U.S.A. distrusted each other. As communist governments took control of Eastern Europe, the Western nations reacted by forming a military alliance called the North Atlantic Treaty Organization (NATO). The frontier between West and East became known as the Iron Curtain.

CONFRONTATION

The Cold War was marked by a series of crises. The first was the Berlin Airlift in 1948, when the West flew in supplies to a Soviet-blockaded Berlin, the former capital of Germany. The superpowers began stockpiling nuclear weapons. Other countries took sides. In 1962, people feared that nuclear war would break out when the United States demanded that the U.S.S.R. withdraw nuclear weapons from Cuba. Eventually, the Soviets backed down and the crisis ended.

THE COLD WAR THAWS

After 1970, tension between the superpowers began to ease. The Cold War finally ended in the 1990s with the fall of communism in many European countries, and the breakup of the Soviet Union.

NO MAN'S LAND

After World War II, Germany was divided. The United States, France, and Britain controlled the West, and the U.S.S.R. controlled the East. The capital, Berlin, was also divided and, from 1949 to 1958, three million people escaped from East to West Berlin. In 1961, East Germany built the Berlin Wall to close off this escape route.

SEE ALSO

Communism, Democracy, Russia and the Baltic States, United States of America, World War II

Color

Color is what we see when light from an object reaches our eyes. White light seems colorless, but it is actually made up of a mixture of colors.

The primary colors of light are red, blue, and green. Mixed together they make up white light.

The primary colors of paint are yellow, blue, and red. Mixed together they produce black.

When you see a rainbow, you are seeing sunlight split apart by raindrops. The rainbow has seven colors: red, orange, yellow, green, blue, indigo, and violet. This range of colors is called the spectrum.

REFLECTING LIGHT

An object only appears to be a particular color because of the light it reflects. For example, a leaf looks green because it reflects green light and absorbs all the other colors in the spectrum.

PRIMARY COLORS

During the 1800s, scientists were amazed to discover that almost any color of light can be created by combining different amounts of a basic set of three colors—red, blue, and green. These are known as the primary colors of light.

MIXING IT UP

If equal amounts of red, blue, and green light are mixed together, they make white light. Mixing just red and green light together makes yellow; blue and green makes cyan (a green-blue); and blue and red makes magenta. In photography, printing, movies, and television, light is mixed to produce millions of different colors.

▲ Georges Seurat's *The Circus* (1891) is painted using a technique called pointillism. Pure color is applied as dots. These merge at a distance to create the subtler shades.

PAINTING A DIFFERENT PICTURE

Pigments (used in paints) have a different set of primary colors. The primary colors are yellow, blue, and red, and when they are mixed together they make black.

SEEING IN COLOR

We see color when light falls on the retina at the back of the eye. The retina is full of cells, called rods and cones, that are sensitive to light. Cones are sensitive to particular colors, and rods, which are not color sensitive, help us to see in dim light.

REFLECTION AND ABSORPTION

When light hits an object, the object absorbs (soaks up) some of the colors of the spectrum and reflects (throws off) others. A tomato, for example, looks red because it reflects red light back into our eyes, but absorbs the other colors of the rainbow: orange, yellow, green, blue, indigo, and violet light.

SEE ALSO

Art, Light, Paint and dye, Printing, Sight, Television, Wavelength

Comet, meteor, and asteroid

Comets, meteors, and asteroids are chunks of ice, rock, or metal that circle the Sun. As they travel closer to Earth, some can be seen lighting up the night sky.

Shooting stars are meteors burning up as they enter Earth's atmosphere.

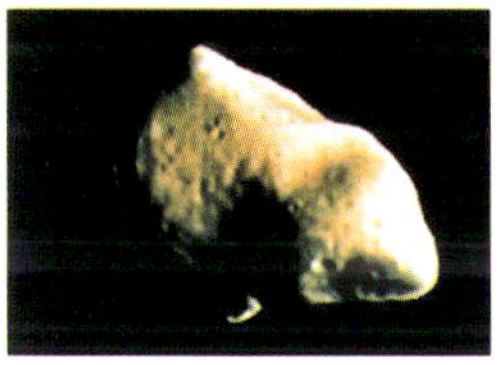

The 12 mi.-long asteroid Gaspra was photographed by the *Galileo* space probe.

Arizona's Barringer Crater was made by a meteorite over 20,000 years ago.

The space between the planets is littered with debris left over from when the solar system formed. Balls of ice and rock with tails are called comets, small particles that blaze through Earth's atmosphere are meteors, and larger chunks of rock and metal are asteroids.

ICE-COLD COMETS

A comet has a fuzzy head and one or more tails. Its head is a lump of ice, dust, and rock, 6–18 mi. (10–30km) across. Surrounding it is a cloud of gas and dust called a coma. The Sun's heat and the solar wind (a stream of particles given off by the Sun) drive dust and gas out from the coma to form the comet's tails.

SHOOTING STARS AND SHOWERS

Many meteors have been around since our solar system formed, but others are chips off comets and asteroids, or even the Moon and Mars. These can be as small as grains of sand and most burn up as they hurtle into Earth's atmosphere at speeds of up to 25 mi./sec. (40km/sec). These are called shooting stars. Some travel in swarms and create a meteor shower in the night sky. Such showers can appear at the same time each year, when Earth crosses the swarm's path. Every year, a few meteors hit Earth's surface and are called meteorites.

THE ASTEROID BELT

Asteroids (sometimes called minor planets) are chunks of rock and metal smaller than planets that circle the Sun. More than 4,000 have been found. The largest asteroid, Ceres, is 580 mi. (930km) across, but most are much smaller. They are usually found in the asteroid belt between Mars and Jupiter.

A COMET IN FLIGHT

Comets are surrounded by clouds of dust, called comas, which can be over 600,000 miles across. Comets travel in long loops around the Sun. Each time they approach the Sun, more gas and dust evaporate from their centers, making the comas grow larger and the comets form tails. Comets' tails always point away from the Sun.

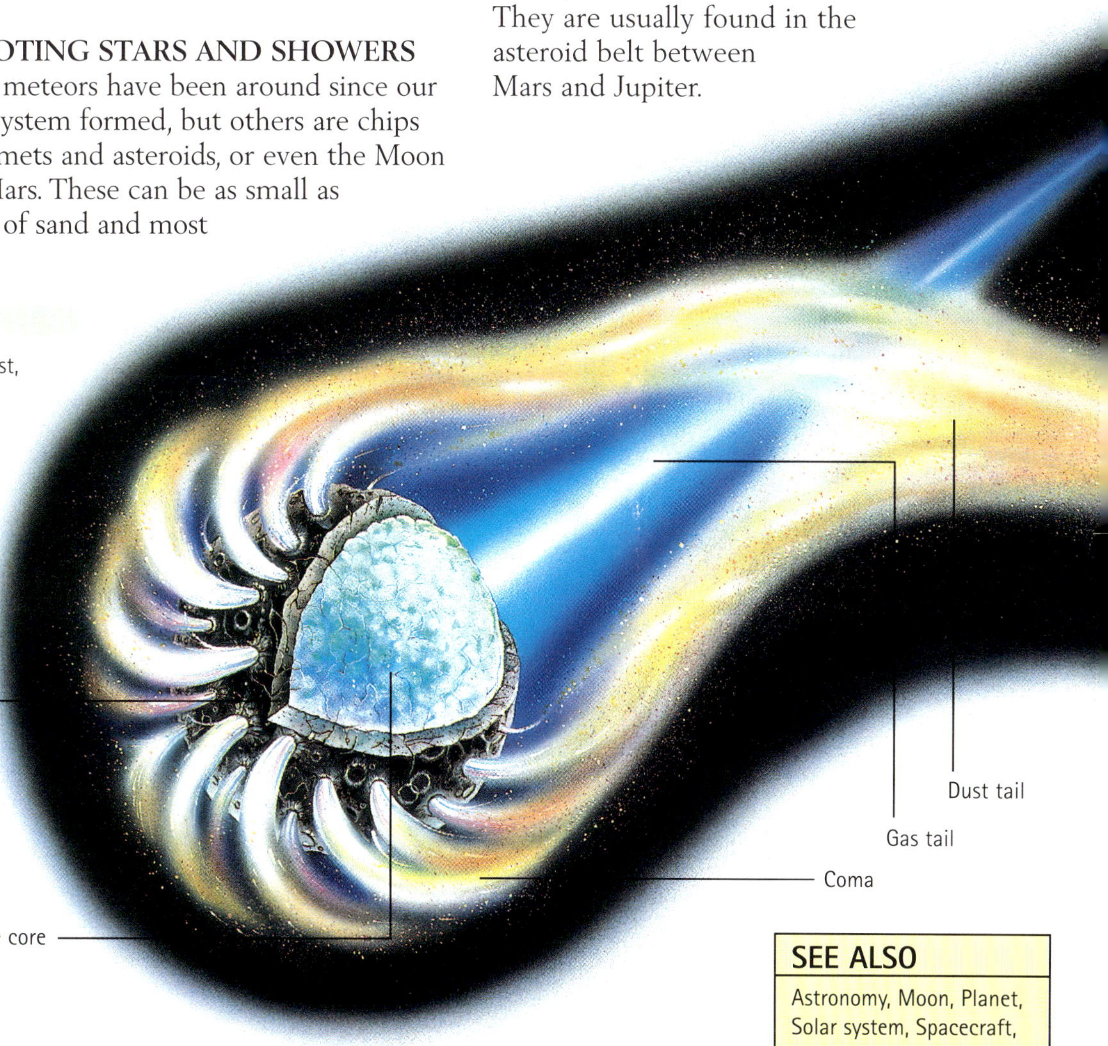

▲ Halley's Comet is visible from Earth every 76 years. It was studied closely on its last return in 1986.

SEE ALSO

Astronomy, Moon, Planet, Solar system, Spacecraft, Space exploration, Sun, Universe

COMMUNICATION

Communication is the process of sending and receiving messages. This can be done by using spoken and written language or recognized signs and signals.

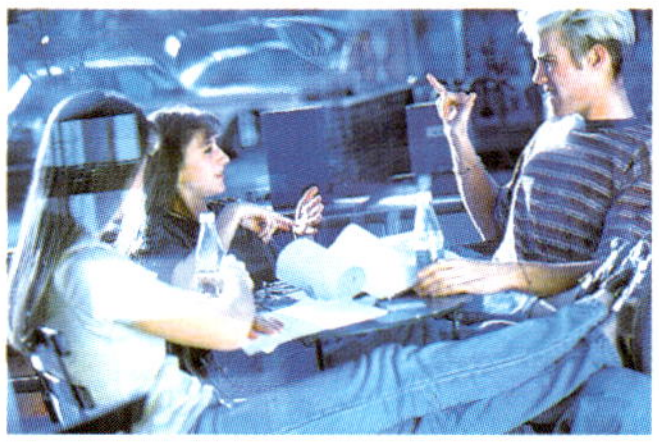

◀ Sign language for the deaf uses hand signals and is based on ideas, not words.

The Sumerians developed the first known writing system in about 3500 B.C.

From the 1400s, printing became a means of mass communication in Europe.

The telephone, invented in 1876, allowed long-distance communication.

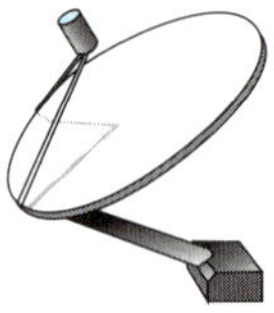

A satellite dish receives images and sounds sent from around the world.

People usually communicate with each other individually or in small groups. However, they sometimes need to relay messages to a much larger audience. This is known as mass communication.

SIGNS AND SIGNALS

Humans have developed ingenious ways of conveying messages to each other, using signs and signals when language cannot be used. Some Native Americans sent smoke signals, and African tribes used drumbeats. Signals are still in use today—navies send messages using flags (known as semaphore), and road users rely on roadside signs and traffic lights.

POSTAL COMMUNICATIONS

One of the earliest, cheapest, and most reliable forms of communication was the mail. Stamps were first used in Britain in 1840. Letters today are sorted by machine, and then carried by truck, train, or airplane to their destination.

TELEGRAPH MESSAGES

For a long time, the fastest way to communicate over long distances was to deliver messages on foot, on horseback, or by boat. Then in 1840, the American inventor Samuel Morse introduced the first simple telegraph, which used electricity to send messages down wire cables. The messages were coded using a system of dots and dashes. This became known as Morse code.

FASTER THAN EVER

Since the 1800s, many inventions, such as the telephone, radio, and television, have made communication across the world faster and easier. Today, a message can be sent to the other side of the world in seconds by using satellite and computer links. The Internet lets all types of computers share services and communicate directly. Video conference centers allow people thousands of miles apart to see and talk to each other directly.

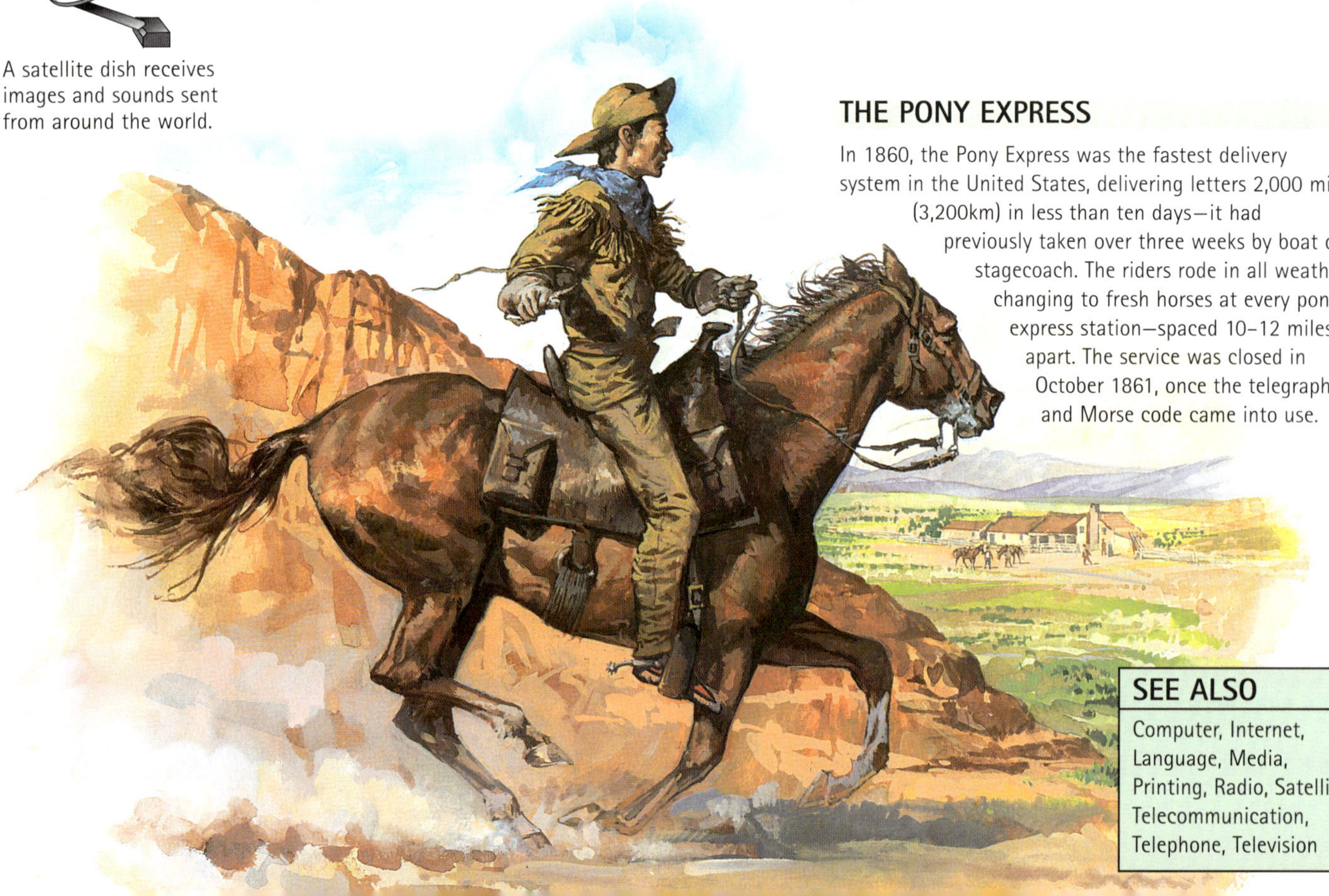

THE PONY EXPRESS

In 1860, the Pony Express was the fastest delivery system in the United States, delivering letters 2,000 mi. (3,200km) in less than ten days—it had previously taken over three weeks by boat or stagecoach. The riders rode in all weather, changing to fresh horses at every pony express station—spaced 10–12 miles apart. The service was closed in October 1861, once the telegraph and Morse code came into use.

SEE ALSO

Computer, Internet, Language, Media, Printing, Radio, Satellite, Telecommunication, Telephone, Television

Communism

Communism is a political theory based on the idea that everybody should share all wealth, property, and industry equally.

The German journalist Karl Marx developed the idea of communism in the 1800s.

In 1848, Karl Marx and Friedrich Engels published the *Communist Manifesto,* which stated that private ownership should be replaced by common ownership. Marx wanted to see an end to the way of life in which most people worked for a low wage, while a few wealthy people owned the factories and land. He believed that the only way to achieve this was by revolution.

Mao Tse-tung led the Communists to victory in China in the 1940s.

THE FIRST REVOLUTION

The first successful communist revolution took place in Russia in 1917, after which the Union of Soviet Socialist Republics (U.S.S.R.) was set up under the leadership of Vladimir Lenin. The state took control of farms, factories, mines, and railroads in the name of the people. Lenin and his successor, Joseph Stalin, ruled as dictators. Most people were better fed and housed, but personal freedoms were severely restricted.

President Fidel Castro has led Cuba since 1959, after a three-year guerrilla war.

SPREAD OF COMMUNISM

After World War II, communism spread to Eastern Europe, China, and countries in Africa, Asia, and Central America. During the Cold War, there was hostile rivalry between communist countries and the United States-led Western democracies.

◀ Since North Korea became communist in 1948, many statues to heroic workers have been erected.

THE COLLAPSE

From 1989 to 1992, communism in countries such as Poland, Hungary, and East Germany collapsed. With the break-up of the Soviet Union in the 1990s, China remains the only major nation with a communist government.

KEY DATES

1848 Journalist Karl Marx and philosopher Friedrich Engels publish the *Communist Manifesto*

1917 Lenin leads Russia's Bolshevik Revolution

1949 China becomes a communist state under Mao Tse-tung

1989 Communism collapses in Eastern Europe

1991 The breakup of the U.S.S.R. leaves only China, Cuba, Vietnam, and North Korea as communist states

Ho Chi Min led North Vietnam for most of the Vietnam War.

► Vladimir Lenin, leader of the Bolshevik Party, led a revolution that overthrew czarist rule in Russia. He set up the world's first communist regime in 1917.

SEE ALSO

China, Cold War, Democracy, Eastern Europe, Europe, Fascism, Revolution, Russia and the Baltic States

COMPUTER

Computers are machines that handle information according to sets of instructions. They then give the results in a form that people can understand.

In 1834, Charles Babbage (1792-1871) designed the first mechanical computer, but he never saw it built.

In the 1960s, computers used transistors and stored data on tape. They could fill a whole room.

The British Sinclair ZX81 was one of the first home computers to be launched on the world market.

Portable laptop computers, small enough to fit inside a briefcase, became available in the 1980s.

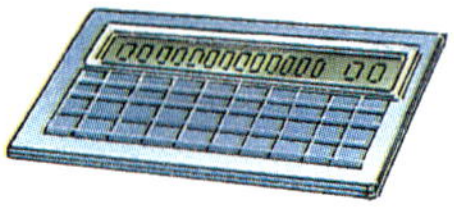

The process of miniaturization created electronic diaries called personal organizers.

The computer is an electronic device that can do calculations millions of times faster than the human brain. First the computer receives data, or information, put in by the user; then it processes the data as simple electrical signals according to its program, and produces a result.

BINARY NUMBERS

All computers use a language called the binary system. Binary numbers are entirely made up of the digits 0 and 1. When a letter is typed on the keyboard or the mouse or joystick is moved, tiny electric currents are sent to the computer. These currents are stored by the computer as binary numbers.

MINIATURIZATION

The first computers took up a whole room, but by the 1960s, electronic components had become much smaller and computers began to shrink in size. The home computer became possible through the invention of the microchip, which contains tens of thousands of electronic components within a space no larger than a fingernail.

KEY WORDS

Bit Binary digit (either a 0 or a 1)

Byte One byte contains eight bits

Hardware The machinery of the computer

Internet Worldwide network of computers

Megabyte One million bytes

Modem Device that connects the computer to the telephone system

Operating system The program that allows the computer to perform general operations

RAM (random-access memory) Used to store programs

ROM (read-only memory) A permanently stored program, such as an operating system (OS)

Software The programs used by the computer

HIGHLY VERSATILE

The PC (personal computer, or micro-computer) can tackle jobs from word processing to 3-D design and animation. Music can be recorded, edited, and played back on the PC. Desktop publishing means that books and magazines can be designed on the PC.

HOW IT WORKS

Data (information) in a PC is usually stored in random-access memory (RAM). The central processing unit (CPU) calls it up when needed, according to a list of instructions (the program) also stored in memory. Data flows to and from the CPU along an electronic pathway called the bus. After processing, data is stored in RAM again.

SCIENCE FRONTIERS

Computers have revolutionized science and technology. Space probes, satellite TV,

HOW THE COMPUTER WORKS

A computer system has four basic parts. An input device such as the keyboard, mouse, or joystick enters information into the computer. Then the central processing unit (CPU), acting as the computer's brain, performs the tasks. The information is sent to an output device, such as the screen or printer, to display the results. And finally a memory unit stores programs and data.

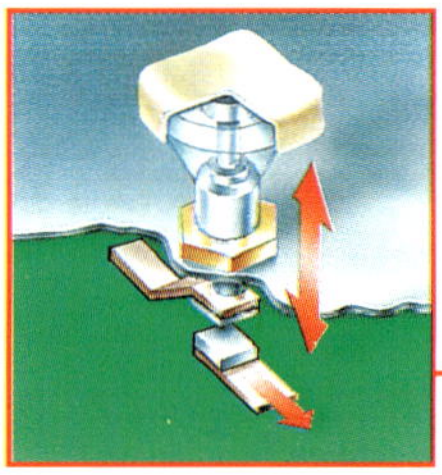

THE KEYBOARD
The keys act as switches, sending tiny electric currents to the computer when pressed.

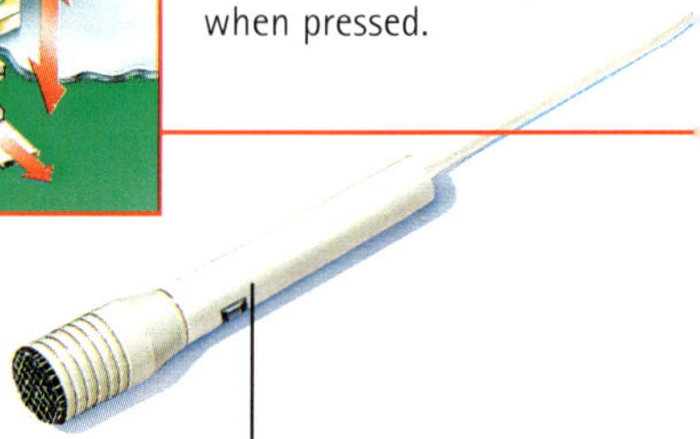

A microphone can be used for recording music, speech, or sound effects directly onto the hard disk

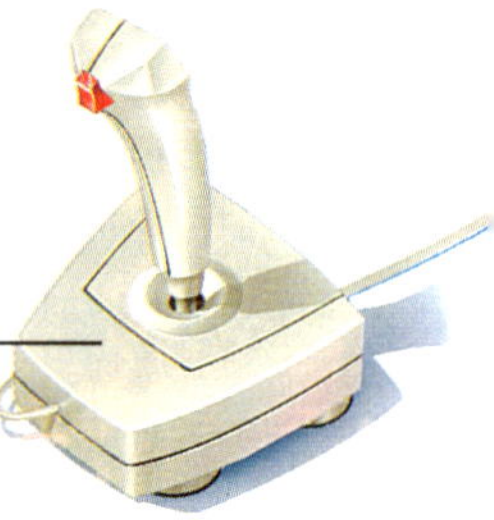

A joystick is used to play computer games

and weapons detection systems all rely on computers. Computers make it possible to test chemical and nuclear reactions without real-life experiments.

AUTOMATION

In the automotive industry, computers are used to design a car and then build it with the aid of robots. In the car itself a computer can check the engine, brakes, and steering. Computers can even be used in the home to control temperature, lighting, and security.

GLOBAL LINKS

Computers are changing the way we live by connecting people and places. The Internet links up computers all over the world, allowing messages and information to be sent across the globe in seconds.

BILL GATES (born 1955)
In 1975, American Bill Gates founded Microsoft, now the largest software company in the world.

▲ Computers contain microchips, like the one shown here. Inside each chip are thousands of electronic parts that store and process electric signals.

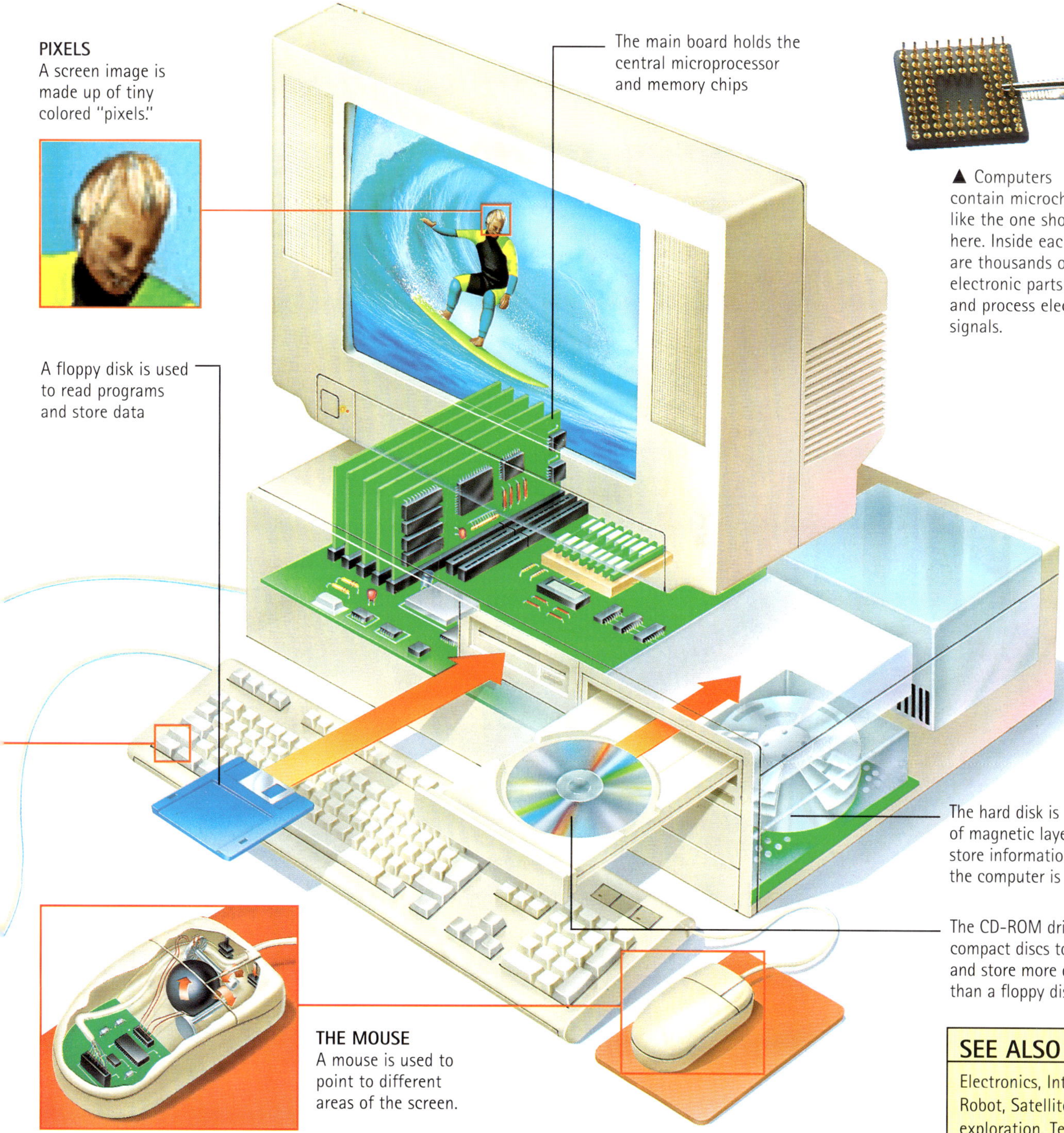

SEE ALSO

Electronics, Internet, Robot, Satellite, Space exploration, Technology, Telecommunication

CONSERVATION

Conservation is the protection and careful use of natural resources, including animals, plants, and fossil fuels. It also includes care of historical treasures.

▲ Recycling plastic, paper, tin, and glass conserves the Earth's resources. In many states, there are laws that specify that households can be fined for failing to separate trash for recycling.

Conservationists try to find a balance between the needs of human beings and care of the environment. There are more than five billion people alive today and they all need land to live on, food to eat, and fuel for power. Without care, habitats can be destroyed, resources used up, and the Earth damaged.

GLOBAL AWARENESS

Some conservation issues are local, as when acres of forest are threatened with felling to make way for a new road. Others, such as recycling, saving energy, and stopping animals from becoming extinct, are shared worldwide. In 1992, world leaders got together at the Earth Summit in Brazil to draw up the very first global action plan to save the planet. One scheme that was introduced to encourage people to stop destroying their habitats—by logging trees or draining marshes—is the "debt-for-nature" idea. This means that a poor country has some of its international debt canceled in exchange for setting aside areas for conservation.

◀ The care and preservation of paintings is a painstaking process. An art conservator must understand a painting's history and content in the same way that an animal conservationist must know the habits of an endangered animal.

FACING EXTINCTION

As many as 100 rare plant and animal species become extinct each day—far more than when the dinosaurs died out, 65 million years ago. The tiger, rhinoceros, Asian snow leopard, and even some species of insects are all in danger of disappearing forever. The last few hundred mountain gorillas live on the borders of Rwanda, Uganda, and Zaire in Africa. Their rain forest home has been destroyed by farmers and timber firms, and they are killed by hungry villagers.

NATURE RESERVES

One of the best ways of protecting wildlife is to preserve an entire habitat in a national park. Zoos also help by breeding rare animals, such as the giant panda.

SAVING THE HELPLESS GIANT

Many species of large whale, such as the humpback whale (below), are threatened with extinction because they have been overhunted for their blubber, meat, oil, and bones. A global conservation body known as the International Whaling Commission (IWC) outlawed the killing of such rare whales in 1985, but not all countries have agreed to stop hunting.

SEE ALSO

Animal, Asia, Dinosaur, Ecology, Energy, Habitat, Pollution, Rain forest, Whale and dolphin, Zoology

Propelled by rocket engines, the supersonic X-15 holds the world air-speed record at 4,520 mph set in 1967.

The funeral mask of the pharaoh Tutankhamen was found in his tomb, discovered in 1922.

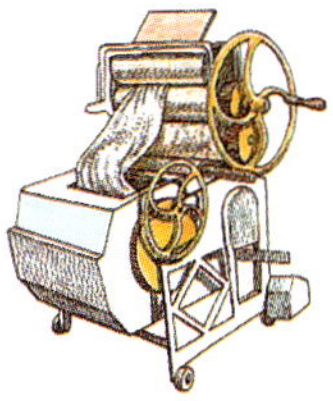

The first washing machine (invented by Hamilton Smith, U.S.A., 1858) still relied on muscle power.

On April 12, 1961, Yuri Gagarin of the U.S.S.R. became the first person in space onboard *Vostok 1*.

The steam gun carriage of 1769, invented by French engineer Cugnot, was the first motorized vehicle.

FACTFINDER

Whether for school projects, or just for fun, this section provides facts, figures, and other essential information—from a world map to presidents and states, and on to biographies of famous figures. It finishes with the highlights of the 20th century. Timelines present key international (top) and U.S. (bottom) developments.

The *chanoyu*, a Japanese tea ceremony which can last four hours, actually originated in China.

In 1834, Charles Babbage (1792-1871) designed the first mechanical computer, but he never saw it built.

The Venus flytrap is a carnivorous plant that feeds on the insects it traps in its leaves.

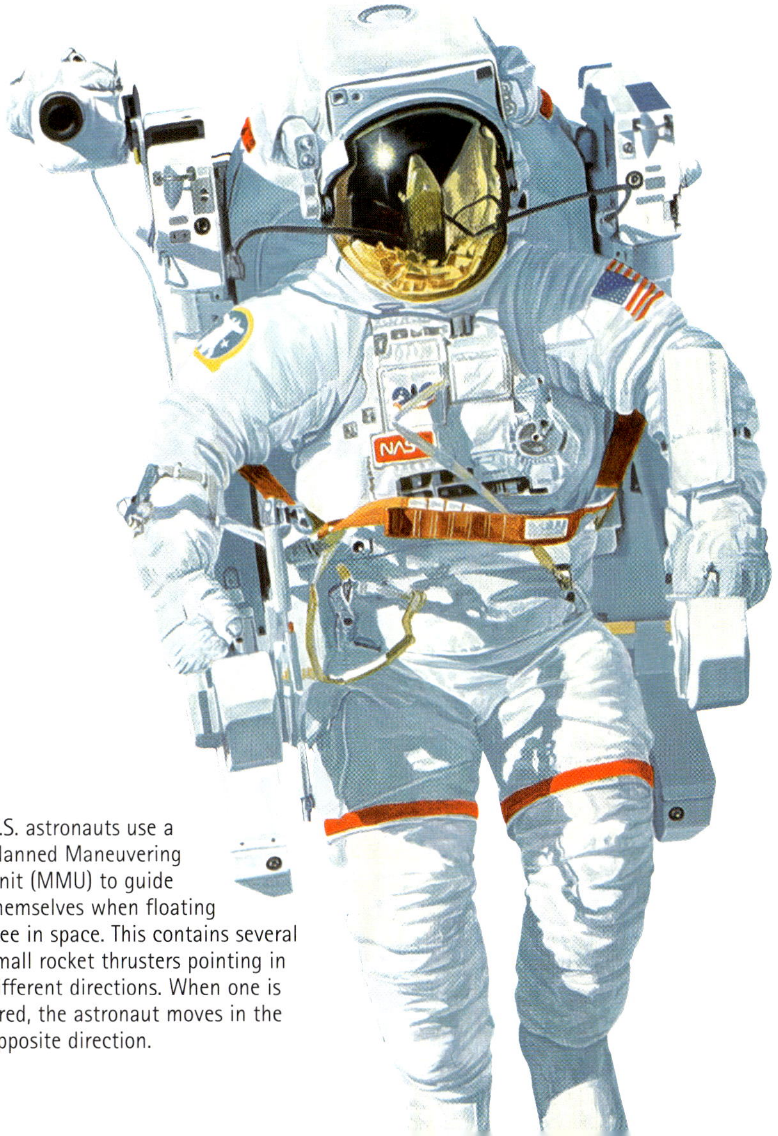

U.S. astronauts use a Manned Maneuvering Unit (MMU) to guide themselves when floating free in space. This contains several small rocket thrusters pointing in different directions. When one is fired, the astronaut moves in the opposite direction.

The Arctic tern is a long-distance flyer, making an annual round trip of up to 25,000 miles.

Camptosaurus was an ornithopod ("bird-footed") dinosaur that lived about 150 million years ago.

Edgar Allan Poe (1809-49) was one of America's greatest poets and an early writer of horror stories.

Countries of the World

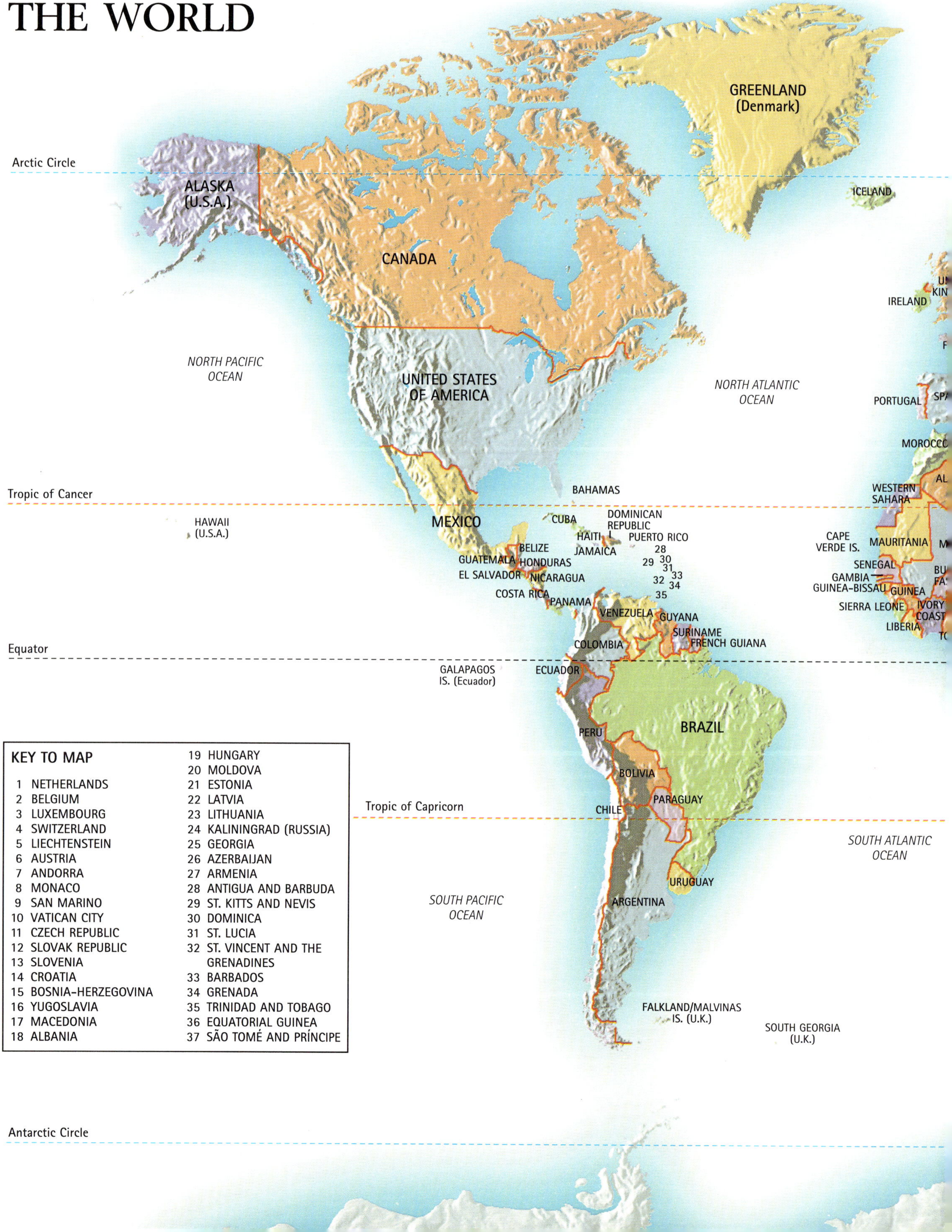

KEY TO MAP

1 NETHERLANDS
2 BELGIUM
3 LUXEMBOURG
4 SWITZERLAND
5 LIECHTENSTEIN
6 AUSTRIA
7 ANDORRA
8 MONACO
9 SAN MARINO
10 VATICAN CITY
11 CZECH REPUBLIC
12 SLOVAK REPUBLIC
13 SLOVENIA
14 CROATIA
15 BOSNIA-HERZEGOVINA
16 YUGOSLAVIA
17 MACEDONIA
18 ALBANIA
19 HUNGARY
20 MOLDOVA
21 ESTONIA
22 LATVIA
23 LITHUANIA
24 KALININGRAD (RUSSIA)
25 GEORGIA
26 AZERBAIJAN
27 ARMENIA
28 ANTIGUA AND BARBUDA
29 ST. KITTS AND NEVIS
30 DOMINICA
31 ST. LUCIA
32 ST. VINCENT AND THE GRENADINES
33 BARBADOS
34 GRENADA
35 TRINIDAD AND TOBAGO
36 EQUATORIAL GUINEA
37 SÃO TOMÉ AND PRÍNCIPE

miles
0
3,000
0
3,000
km
ARCTIC OCEAN
RUSSIA
SWEDEN
FINLAND
21
22
23
24
MARK
MANY
POLAND
BELARUS
UKRAINE
11
12
6
19
20
13
14
ROMANIA
15
16
9
17
BULGARIA
18
GREECE
MALTA
TURKEY
25
26
27
CYPRUS
SYRIA
LEBANON
ISRAEL
JORDAN
IRAQ
IRAN
KUWAIT
BAHRAIN
QATAR
UNITED ARAB EMIRATES
SAUDI ARABIA
OMAN
YEMEN
LIBYA
EGYPT
CHAD
SUDAN
ERITREA
DJIBOUTI
ETHIOPIA
SOMALI REPUBLIC
CENTRAL AFRICAN REP.
REP. OF CONGO
DEM. REP. OF CONGO
UGANDA
KENYA
RWANDA
BURUNDI
TANZANIA
ANGOLA
ZAMBIA
MALAWI
ZIMBABWE
MOZAMBIQUE
NAMIBIA
BOTSWANA
SWAZILAND
SOUTH AFRICA
LESOTHO
MADAGASCAR
COMOROS
SEYCHELLES
MAURITIUS
REUNION (Fr.)
KAZAKHSTAN
UZBEKISTAN
TURKMENISTAN
KYRGYZSTAN
TAJIKISTAN
AFGHANISTAN
PAKISTAN
INDIA
NEPAL
BHUTAN
BANGLADESH
SRI LANKA
MALDIVES
MONGOLIA
CHINA
NORTH KOREA
SOUTH KOREA
JAPAN
TAIWAN
MYANMAR (BURMA)
LAOS
VIETNAM
THAILAND
CAMBODIA
PHILIPPINES
MALAYSIA
SINGAPORE
INDONESIA
PAPUA NEW GUINEA
PALAU
FED. STATES OF MICRONESIA
MARSHALL IS.
KIRIBATI
NAURU
TUVALU
SOLOMON IS.
WESTERN SAMOA
VANUATU
FIJI
NEW CALEDONIA (Fr.)
NORTH PACIFIC OCEAN
INDIAN OCEAN
AUSTRALIA
NEW ZEALAND
ANTARCTICA

c. 9000 B.C.

Agriculture develops in Middle East

c. 3500 B.C.
First cities appear in Sumeria; writing invented

c. 3100 B.C.
Upper and Lower Egypt united

c. 2500 B.C.
Indus Valley civilization in Pakistan

2300s B.C.
Mesopotamia, world's first empire, flourishes

STATES OF THE UNITED STATES

STATE	CAPITAL	POPULATION (1997 ESTIMATE)	(RANK)	AREA (IN SQ. MI.)	(RANK)	ENTRY INTO UNION	(ORDER)
Alabama	Montgomery	4,319,000	(23)	52,423	(30)	December 14, 1819	(22)
Alaska	Juneau	609,000	(48)	656,424	(1)	January 3, 1959	(49)
Arizona	Phoenix	4,555,000	(21)	114,006	(6)	February 14, 1912	(48)
Arkansas	Little Rock	2,523,000	(33)	53,182	(29)	June 15, 1836	(25)
California	Sacramento	32,268,000	(1)	163,707	(3)	September 9, 1850	(31)
Colorado	Denver	3,893,000	(25)	104,100	(8)	August 1, 1876	(38)
Connecticut	Hartford	3270,000	(28)	5,544	(48)	January 9, 1788	(5)
Delaware	Dover	732,000	(46)	2,489	(49)	December 7, 1787	(1)
Florida	Tallahassee	14,654,000	(4)	65,758	(22)	March 3, 1845	(27)
Georgia	Atlanta	7,486,000	(10)	59,441	(24)	January 2, 1788	(4)
Hawaii	Honolulu	1,187,000	(41)	10,932	(43)	August 21, 1959	(50)
Idaho	Boise	1,210,000	(40)	83,574	(14)	July 3, 1890	(43)
Illinois	Springfield	11,896,000	(6)	57,918	(25)	December 3, 1818	(21)
Indiana	Indianapolis	5,864,000	(14)	36,420	(38)	December 11, 1816	(19)
Iowa	Des Moines	2,852,000	(30)	56,276	(26)	December 28, 1846	(29)
Kansas	Topeka	2,595,000	(32)	82,282	(15)	January 29, 1861	(34)
Kentucky	Frankfort	3,908,000	(24)	40,411	(37)	June 1, 1792	(15)
Louisiana	Baton Rouge	4,352,000	(22)	51,843	(31)	April 30, 1812	(18)
Maine	Augusta	1,242,000	(39)	35,387	(39)	March 15, 1820	(23)
Maryland	Annapolis	5,094,000	(19)	12,407	(42)	April 28, 1788	(7)
Massachusetts	Boston	6,118,000	(13)	10,555	(44)	February 6, 1788	(6)
Michigan	Lansing	9,774,000	(8)	96,705	(11)	January 26, 1837	(26)
Minnesota	St. Paul	4,686,000	(20)	86,943	(12)	May 11, 1858	(32)
Mississippi	Jackson	2,731,000	(31)	48,434	(32)	December 10, 1817	(20)
Missouri	Jefferson City	5,402,000	(16)	69,709	(21)	August 10, 1821	(24)
Montana	Helena	879,000	(44)	147,046	(4)	November 8, 1889	(41)
Nebraska	Lincoln	1,657,000	(38)	77,358	(16)	March 1, 1867	(37)
Nevada	Carson City	1,677,000	(37)	110,567	(7)	October 31, 1864	(36)
New Hampshire	Concord	1,173,000	(42)	9,351	(46)	June 21, 1788	(9)
New Jersey	Trenton	8,053,000	(9)	8,722	(47)	December 18, 1787	(3)
New Mexico	Santa Fe	1,730,000	(36)	121,598	(5)	January 6, 1912	(47)
New York	Albany	18,137,000	(3)	54,556	(27)	July 26, 1788	(11)
North Carolina	Raleigh	7,425,000	(11)	53,821	(28)	November 21, 1789	(12)
North Dakota	Bismarck	641,000	(47)	70,704	(19)	November 2, 1889	(39)
Ohio	Columbus	11,186,000	(7)	44,828	(34)	March 1, 1803	(17)
Oklahoma	Oklahoma City	3,317,000	(27)	69,903	(20)	November 16, 1907	(46)
Oregon	Salem	3,243,000	(29)	98,386	(9)	February 14, 1859	(33)
Pennsylvania	Harrisburg	12,020,000	(5)	46,058	(33)	December 12, 1787	(2)
Rhode Island	Providence	987,000	(43)	1,545	(50)	May 29, 1790	(13)
South Carolina	Columbia	3,760,000	(26)	32,008	(40)	May 23, 1788	(8)
South Dakota	Pierre	738,000	(45)	77,121	(17)	November 2, 1889	(40)
Tennessee	Nashville	5,368,000	(17)	42,146	(36)	June 1, 1796	(16)
Texas	Austin	19,439,000	(2)	268,601	(2)	December 29, 1845	(28)
Utah	Salt Lake City	2,059,000	(34)	84,904	(13)	January 4, 1896	(45)
Vermont	Montpelier	589,000	(49)	9,615	(45)	March 4, 1791	(14)
Virginia	Richmond	6,734,000	(12)	42,777	(35)	June 25, 1788	(10)
Washington	Olympia	5,610,000	(15)	71,302	(18)	November 11, 1889	(42)
West Virginia	Charleston	1,816,000	(35)	24,231	(41)	June 20, 1863	(35)
Wisconsin	Madison	5,170,000	(18)	65,499	(23)	May 29, 1848	(30)
Wyoming	Cheyenne	480,000	(50)	97,818	(10)	July 10, 1890	(44)

American Indian ancestors arrive from Asia
38 000 B.C.–8000 B.C.

Folsom culture in the Great Plains
9000 B.C.–8000 B.C.

Olmec civilization in Mexico and Central America
1200 B.C.–100 B.C.

Maya civilization in Central America
A.D. 300–900

Mound Builders in Mississippi Valley
700

Vikings explore NE coast of North America
1000

c. 1792–50 B.C. King Hammurabi rules Babylonia

800–600 B.C. Assyrian Empire

551 B.C. Birth of Confucius

500–323 B.C. Golden Age of Greece

563 B.C. Birth of Buddha

331 B.C. Alexander the Great conquers Persian Empire

PRESIDENTS OF THE UNITED STATES

	NAME (PARTY)*	BIRTH-DEATH DATES	TERM IN OFFICE	VICE PRESIDENT(S)
1.	George Washington *(F)*	1732 – 1799	Apr. 30, 1789 – Mar. 4, 1797	John Adams
2.	John Adams *(F)*	1735 – 1826	Mar. 4, 1797 – Mar. 4, 1801	Thomas Jefferson
3.	Thomas Jefferson *(D–R)*	1743 – 1826	Mar. 4, 1801 – Mar. 4, 1809	Aaron Burr
				George Clinton
4.	James Madison *(D–R)*	1751 – 1836	Mar. 4, 1809 – Mar. 4, 1817	George Clinton
				Elbridge Gerry
5.	James Monroe *(D–R)*	1758 – 1831	Mar. 4, 1817 – Mar. 4, 1825	Daniel D. Tompkins
6.	John Quincy Adams *(D–R)*	1767 – 1848	Mar. 4, 1825 – Mar. 4, 1829	John C. Calhoun
7.	Andrew Jackson *(D)*	1767 – 1845	Mar. 4, 1829 – Mar. 4, 1837	John C. Calhoun,
				Martin Van Buren
8.	Martin Van Buren *(D)*	1782 – 1862	Mar. 4, 1837 – Mar. 4, 1841	Richard M. Johnson
9.	William Henry Harrison *(W)*	1773 – 1841	Mar. 4, 1841 – Apr. 4, 1841	John Tyler
10.	John Tyler *(W)*	1790 – 1862	Apr. 4, 1841 – Mar. 4, 1845	–
11.	James K. Polk *(D)*	1795 – 1849	Mar. 4, 1845 – Mar. 4, 1849	George M. Dallas
12.	Zachary Taylor *(W)*	1784 – 1850	Mar. 4, 1849 – July 9, 1850	Millard Fillmore
13	Millard Fillmore *(W)*	1800 – 1874	July 9, 1850 – Mar. 4, 1853	–
14.	Franklin Pierce *(D)*	1804 – 1869	Mar. 4, 1853 – Mar. 4, 1857	William R. King
15.	James Buchanan *(D)*	1791 – 1868	Mar. 4, 1857 – Mar. 4, 1861	John C. Breckinridge
16.	Abraham Lincoln *(R)*	1809 – 1865	Mar. 4, 1861 – Apr. 15, 1865	Hannibal Hamlin,
				Andrew Johnson
17.	Andrew Johnson *(R)*	1808 – 1875	Apr. 15, 1865 – Mar. 4, 1869	–
18.	Ulysses S. Grant *(R)*	1822 – 1885	Mar. 4, 1869 – Mar. 4, 1877	Schuyler Colfax
				Henry Wilson
19.	Rutherford B. Hayes *(R)*	1822 – 1893	Mar. 4, 1877 – Mar. 4, 1881	William A. Wheeler
20.	James A. Garfield *(R)*	1831 – 1881	Mar. 4, 1881 – Sept. 19, 1881	Chester A. Arthur
21.	Chester A. Arthur *(R)*	1829 – 1886	Sept. 19, 1881 – Mar. 4, 1885	–
22.	Grover Cleveland *(D)*	1837 – 1908	Mar. 4, 1885 – Mar. 4, 1889	Thomas A. Hendricks
23.	Benjamin Harrison *(R)*	1833 – 1901	Mar. 4, 1889 – Mar. 4, 1893	Levi P. Morton
24.	Grover Cleveland *(D)*	1837 – 1908	Mar. 4, 1893 – Mar. 4, 1897	Adlai E. Stevenson
25.	William McKinley *(R)*	1843 – 1901	Mar. 4, 1897 – Sept. 14, 1901	Garret A. Hobart
				Theodore Roosevelt
26.	Theodore Roosevelt *(R)*	1858 – 1919	Sept. 14, 1901 – Mar. 4, 1909	Charles W. Fairbanks
27.	William H. Taft *(R)*	1857 – 1930	Mar. 4, 1909 – Mar. 4, 1913	James S. Sherman
28.	Woodrow Wilson *(D)*	1856 – 1924	Mar. 4, 1913 – Mar. 4, 1921	Thomas R. Marshall
29.	Warren G. Harding *(R)*	1865 – 1923	Mar. 4, 1921 – Aug. 2, 1923	Calvin Coolidge
30.	Calvin Coolidge *(R)*	1872 – 1933	Aug. 3, 1923 – Mar. 4, 1929	Charles G. Dawes
31.	Herbert Hoover *(R)*	1874 – 1964	Mar. 4, 1929 – Mar. 4, 1933	Charles Curtis
32.	Franklin D. Roosevelt *(D)*	1882 – 1945	Mar. 4, 1933 – Apr. 12, 1945	John N. Garner
				Henry A. Wallace
				Harry S. Truman
33.	Harry S. Truman *(D)*	1884 – 1972	Apr. 12, 1945 – Jan. 20, 1953	Alben W. Barkley
34.	Dwight D. Eisenhower *(R)*	1890 – 1969	Jan. 20, 1953 – Jan. 20, 1961	Richard M. Nixon
35.	John F. Kennedy *(D)*	1917 – 1963	Jan. 20, 1961 – Nov. 22, 1963	Lyndon B. Johnson
36.	Lyndon B. Johnson *(D)*	1908 – 1973	Nov. 22, 1963 – Jan. 20, 1969	Hubert H. Humphrey
37.	Richard M. Nixon *(R)*	1913 – 1994	Jan. 20, 1969 – Aug. 9, 1974	Spiro T. Agnew
				Gerald R. Ford
38.	Gerald R. Ford *(R)*	1913 –	Aug. 9, 1974 – Jan. 20, 1977	Nelson A. Rockefeller
39.	Jimmy Carter *(D)*	1924 –	Jan. 20, 1977 – Jan. 20, 1981	Walter F. Mondale
40.	Ronald Reagan *(R)*	1911 –	Jan. 20, 1981 – Jan. 20, 1989	George Bush
41.	George Bush *(R)*	1924 –	Jan. 20, 1989 – Jan. 20, 1993	Dan Quayle
42.	Bill Clinton *(D)*	1946 –	Jan. 20, 1993 –	Al Gore

*Federalist (*F*), Whig (*W*), Democratic-Republican (*D–R*), Republican (*R*), Democrat (*D*)

George Washington refused a third term as the first U.S. President.

Abraham Lincoln was the first president assassinated in office.

Franklin D. Roosevelt led the U.S. during the Depression and WWII.

John F. Kennedy symbolized the young spirit of the 1960s.

1400 Aztec Empire in Mexico

Late 1400s Inca Empire flourishes in Andes

1492 Columbus "discovers" Western Hemisphere

1497 John Cabot explores NE coast of North America

1521 Spanish conquer Aztecs

1540–42 Francisco Coronado explores American SW

1565 St. Augustine (Florida) founded by Spaniards

c. A.D. 30	117	c. 320	500s	622	c. 800	868
Jesus Christ crucified	Height of Roman Empire	Hindu Gupta Dynasty flourishes in India	Byzantine Empire at peak	Muhammad's flight: Islam established	Kingdom of Ghana in Africa at peak	China makes first printed book

The Statue of Liberty welcomes all who enter New York Harbor.

Sir John A. MacDonald led the first government of Canada as a Dominion.

POPULATION OF LARGEST AMERICAN CITIES (1996 estimate)

RANK	CITY	POPULATION	RANK	CITY	POPULATION	RANK	CITY	POPULATION
1.	New York City, NY	7,380,906	26.	Denver, CO	497,840	51.	Mesa, AZ	344,764
2.	Los Angeles, CA	3,553,638	27.	Portland, OR	480,824	52.	Wichita, KS	320,395
3.	Chicago, IL	2,721,547	28.	Fort Worth, TX	479,716	53.	Toledo, OH	317,606
4.	Houston, TX	1,744,058	29.	New Orleans, LA	476,625	54.	Buffalo, NY	310,548
5.	Philadelphia, PA	1,478,002	30.	Oklahoma City, OK	469,852	55.	Santa Ana, CA	302,419
6.	San Diego, CA	1,171,121	31.	Tucson, AZ	449,002	56.	Arlington, TX	294,816
7.	Phoenix, AZ	1,159,014	32.	Charlotte, NC	441,297	57.	Anaheim, CA	288,945
8.	San Antonio, TX	1,067,816	33.	Kansas City, MO	441,259	58.	Tampa, FL	285,206
9.	Dallas, TX	1,053,292	34.	Virginia Beach, VA	430,385	59.	Corpus Christi, TX	280,260
10.	Detroit, MI	1,000,272	35.	Honolulu, HI	423,475	60.	Newark, NJ	268,510
11.	San Jose, CA	838,744	36.	Long Beach, CA	421,904	61.	Louisville, KY	260,689
12.	Indianapolis, IN	746,737	37.	Albuquerque, NM	419,681	62.	St. Paul, MN	259,606
13.	San Francisco, CA	735,315	38.	Atlanta, GA	401,907	63.	Birmingham, AL	258,543
14.	Jacksonville, FL	679,792	39.	Fresno, CA	396,011	64.	Riverside, CA	255,069
15.	Baltimore, MD	675,401	40.	Tulsa, OK	378,491	65.	Aurora, CO	252,341
16.	Columbus, OH	657,053	41.	Las Vegas, NV	376,906	66.	Anchorage, AK	250,505
17.	El Paso, TX	599,865	42.	Sacramento, CA	376,243	67.	Raleigh, NC	243,835
18.	Memphis, TN	596,725	43.	Oakland, CA	367,230	68.	Lexington-Fayette, KY	239,942
19.	Milwaukee, WI	590,503	44.	Miami, FL	365,127	69.	St. Petersburg, FL	235,988
20.	Boston, MA	558,394	45.	Omaha, NE	364,253	70.	Norfolk, VA	233,430
21.	Washington, DC	543,213	46.	Minneapolis, MN	358,785	71.	Stockton, CA	232,660
22.	Austin, TX	541,278	47.	St. Louis, MO	351,565	72.	Jersey City, NJ	229,039
23.	Seattle, WA	524,704	48.	Pittsburgh, PA	350,363	73.	Rochester, NY	221,594
24.	Nashville-Davidson, TN	511,263	49.	Cincinnati, OH	345,818	74.	Akron, OH	216,882
25.	Cleveland, OH	498,246	50.	Colorado Springs, CO	345,127	75.	Baton Rouge, LA	215,882

THE PROVINCES AND TERRITORIES OF CANADA

PROVINCES	CAPITAL	POPULATION (1996 CENSUS)	(RANK)	AREA IN SQ. MI.	(RANK)	DATE BECAME PROVINCE
Alberta	Edmonton	2,696,826	(4)	255,287	(4)	1905
British Columbia	Victoria	3,724,500	(3)	365,900	(3)	1871
Manitoba	Winnipeg	1,113,898	(5)	250,947	(6)	1870
New Brunswick	Fredericton	738,133	(8)	28,355	(8)	1867
Newfoundland	St. John's	551,792	(9)	156,649	(7)	1949
Nova Scotia	Halifax	909,282	(7)	21,425	(9)	1867
Ontario	Toronto	10,753,573	(1)	412,581	(2)	1867
Prince Edward Island	Charlottetown	134,557	(10)	2,185	(10)	1873
Quebec	Quebec	7,138,795	(2)	594,860	(1)	1867
Saskatchewan	Regina	990,237	(6)	251,866	(5)	1905

TERRITORIES	CAPITAL	POPULATION (1996 CENSUS)	AREA IN SQ. MI.
Northwest Territories	Yellowknife	64,402	1,322,910
Yukon Territory	Whitehorse	30,766	186,661

PRIME MINISTERS OF CANADA

NAME	SERVED	POLITCAL PARTY
Sir John A. Macdonald	1867–1873	Conservative
Alexander Mackenzie	1873–1878	Liberal
Sir John A. Macdonald	1878–1891	Convervative
Sir John Abbott	1891–1892	Conservative
Sir John Thompson	1892–1894	Conservative
Sir Mackenzie Bowell	1894–1896	Conservative
Sir Charles Tupper	1896	Conservative
Sir Wilfrid Laurier	1896–1911	Liberal
Sir Robert Borden	1911–1917	Conservative
Sir Robert Borden	1917–1920	Unionist
Arthur Meighen	1920–1921	Unionist
W.L. Mackenzie King	1921–1926	Liberal
Arthur Meighen	1926	Conservative
W.L. Mackenzie King	1926–1930	Liberal
Richard Bennett	1930–1935	Conservative
W.L. Mackenzie King	1935–1948	Liberal
Louis St. Laurent	1948–1957	Liberal
John Diefenbaker	1957–1963	Progressive Conservative
Lester B. Pearson	1963–1968	Liberal
Pierre E. Trudeau	1968–1979	Liberal
Charles Joseph Clark	1979–1980	Progressive Conservative
Pierre E. Trudeau	1980–1984	Liberal
John Turner	1984	Liberal
Brian Mulroney	1984–1993	Progressive Conservative
Kim Campbell	1993	Progressive Conservative
Jean Chrétien	1993–	Liberal

1607	1620	1626	1634	1636	1664
First British settlement: Jamestown, VA	Pilgrims found colony at Plymouth, MA	Dutch establish city of New Amsterdam	Colony of Maryland founded	Roger Williams founds Providence, RI	English seize New Amsterdam, rename it New York

1260s
Mongol Empire at peak

1300
Start of Renaissance

1307
Height of Mali Empire in Africa

1492
Columbus sails to New World

1500s
Reformation; birth of Protestantism

1522
Magellan's ship first to sail around the world

1526
Mogul Empire founded in India

INTERNATIONAL ORGANIZATIONS

United Nations (UN)
was founded in 1945. Its goals are to maintain international peace and security, and solve cultural, social, and humanitarian problems. There were 51 original members of the UN; in 1997 there were 185 members. Headquarters: New York City. The UN's main organs include: the General Assembly, with representatives of all members; the Security Council, with 15 members, 5 of whom (China, France, Russia, U.K., and U.S.) have permanent seats and 10 of whom are elected for 2 years; and the International Court of Justice, or World Court, which sits in The Hague, Netherlands.

Following are eight of the UN's specialized and related agencies:

Food and Agriculture Organization (FAO)
helps improve production and distribution of food and world dietary standards. Headquarters: Rome, Italy.

International Bank for Reconstruction and Development (IBRD),
or World Bank, provides loans and technical help for economic projects in developing countries. Headquarters: Washington, D.C.

International Monetary Fund (IMF)
promotes monetary cooperation and the expansion of world trade. Headquarters: Washington, D.C.

United Nations Children's Fund (UNICEF)
helps children in developing nations. Headquarters: New York City.

United Nations Educational, Scientific, and Cultural Organization (UNESCO)
promotes exchange of information, ideas, and culture. Headquarters: Paris, France.

United Nations High Commissioner for Refugees (UNHCR)
provides assistance to refugees worldwide. It is based in Geneva, Switzerland.

World Health Organization (WHO)
fights disease and helps improve health standards. Headquarters: Geneva, Switzerland.

World Trade Organization (WTO)
administers trade agreements and attempts to settle disputes. Headquarters: Geneva, Switzerland.

Other international organizations include:

Caribbean Community and Common Market (CARICOM)
was founded in 1973. Members are Antigua and Barbuda, Bahamas, Barbados, Belize, Dominica, Grenada, Guyana, Jamaica, Montserrat, St. Kitts and Nevis, St. Lucia, St. Vincent and the Grenadines, Suriname, and Trinidad and Tobago. Headquarters: Georgetown, Guyana.

The Commonwealth,
founded in 1949, is a loose association of Great Britain and more than 50 other nations that were once part of the British Empire. Mozambique, the most recent member, had not been part of the British Empire. Headquarters: London, England.

Commonwealth of Independent States (CIS),
founded in 1991, is made up of 12 of the 15 former Soviet republics. Members are Armenia, Azerbaijan, Belarus, Georgia, Kazakhstan, Kyrgyzstan, Moldova, Russia, Tajikistan, Turkmenistan, Ukraine, and Uzbekistan. Headquarters: Minsk, Belarus.

European Union (EU),
founded in 1952 with 6 members, was originally a free-trade and customs union. It is now a closer political and economic union. Members are Austria, Belgium, Denmark, Finland, France, Germany, Greece, Ireland, Italy, Luxembourg, the Netherlands, Portugal, Spain, Sweden, and the U.K.

Group of Eight (G-8),
is a group of eight leading industrialized nations that meet to discuss economic issues. Until Russia was admitted in 1997, it was known as the Group of Seven (G-7). The original members are Canada, France, Germany, Japan, Italy, the U.K., and the U.S.

International Criminal Police Organization (Interpol),
founded in 1956, promotes cooperation between police authorities in 177 countries. Headquarters: Lyon, France.

League of Arab States,
also known as the Arab League; promotes economic, social, political, and military cooperation among members. Founded in 1945, it has 22 members, including Palestine, which it considers an independent nation. Headquarters: Cairo, Egypt.

North Atlantic Treaty Organization (NATO)
is a military alliance of Western nations. It was founded in 1949 to defend Western Europe, the U.S., and Canada from military aggression. Members are Belgium, Canada, Denmark, France, Germany, Greece, Iceland, Italy, Luxembourg, the Netherlands, Norway, Portugal, Spain, Turkey, the U.K., and the U.S. Beginning in 1997, plans were made to admit some former Eastern European communist nations into NATO. Headquarters: Brussels, Belgium.

Organization for Economic Cooperation and Development (OECD)
was founded in 1961. Its goals are to promote economic growth, financial stability, and social welfare in its 29 member nations and to assist developing nations. Headquarters: Paris, France.

Organization of African Unity (OAU)
was founded in 1963 to promote unity and cooperation among African nations. It has 53 members. Headquarters: Addis Ababa, Ethiopia.

Organization of American States (OAS)
was founded in 1948. Its major goal is the peaceful settlement of disputes between nations. It has 35 members. Cuba has been suspended from OAS activities since 1962, but not from membership. Headquarters: Washington, D.C.

Organization of Petroleum Exporting Countries (OPEC)
was founded in 1960 to coordinate oil production and prices. Members are Algeria, Indonesia, Iran, Iraq, Kuwait, Libya, Nigeria, Qatar, Saudi Arabia, United Arab Emirates, and Venezuela. Headquarters: Vienna, Austria.

Logo for the League of Arab States, which mediates disputes among its member nations.

Logo for the European Union. This was known as the European Community (EC) until 1994.

The Commonwealth of Independent States is not in itself a state but an alliance of fully independent states.

Since the end of the Cold War in the 1990s, NATO has had to reassess its military role.

French and Indian War ends
1763

First Continental Congress
1774

Revolutionary War begins
1775

Declaration of Independence
1776

Americans defeat British at Yorktown, VA
1781

Revolutionary War officially ends
1783

U.S. Constitution adopted
1788

1618–48 Thirty Years' War

1644 Start of Manchu rule in China

1700s–1800s Industrial Revolution

1756–63 Seven Years' War

1775–83 Revolutionary War

1789–99 French Revolution

1804–15 Napoleonic Wars

1811–25 Latin American nations win independence

BIOGRAPHIES

Leonardo was not only an artist, but also an inventor, mathematician, engineer, and anatomist.

Picasso was the most famous artist of the 20th century. His work changed the course of modern art.

Chaucer's *Canterbury Tales* is a collection of stories told by pilgrims on their journey to Canterbury.

Brought up in poverty himself, Dickens wrote knowledgeably about the lives of the poor.

ARTISTS

Audubon, John James (1785-1851), a U.S. artist and naturalist, was noted for his paintings of birds.

Botticelli, Sandro (c.1445-1510) was an Italian painter. Works such as *Primavera* (Spring) and the *Birth of Venus* reflect the humanist and classical interests of his time.

Copley, John Singleton (1738-1815) is considered the greatest painter of colonial America. He painted portraits of people such as Paul Revere in natural poses.

Cézanne, Paul (1839-1906), a French painter, started out as an impressionist. His paintings showed the effects of light on objects rather than the objects themselves. He later painted colorful, more solid forms.

Degas, Edgar (1834-1917), a French painter and sculptor, was influenced by impressionism and Japanese woodcuts. He was interested in the human form, and many of his subjects were ballet dancers. His paintings include *The Rehearsal* and *Dance Class.*

Giotto (c.1266-1337), an Italian painter, revived the art of painting in the early Renaissance period. He was especially known for his religious frescoes, including *Life of Christ* and the *Last Judgment.*

Goya y Lucientes, Francisco José de (1746-1828), a Spaniard, painted realistic portraits and scenes from everyday life, including *The Disasters of War.*

Hopper, Edward (1882-1967) painted ordinary American scenes. The people in many of his paintings are often shown as lonely or sad.

Homer, Winslow (1836-1910) is considered one of the greatest U.S. artists. His paintings, including *Breezing Up* and *Gulf Stream*, captured the power and beauty of the sea.

Leonardo da Vinci (1452-1519), an Italian painter and scientist, was a genius. His greatest works include the *Last Supper* and the *Mona Lisa.*

Michelangelo (1475-1564), an Italian painter, sculptor, and architect, created the frescoes on the ceiling of the Sistine Chapel and sculptures of the *Pietà* and *David.*

Monet, Claude (1840-1926), a French painter, was one of the creators of the impressionist movement. Among his most famous works are *Impression: Sunrise*, the Rouen Cathedral series, and the Water Lily series.

Picasso, Pablo (1881-1973), a Spaniard, is thought by many to be the greatest artist of the 20th century. With Georges Braque, he developed cubism, a style in which forms are broken down into geometric shapes.

Pollock, Jackson (1912-56), an American, one of the most influential artists of the 20th century, was an abstract expressionist who made the colors and shapes of his paintings reflect his feelings. Among his works are *Autumn Rhythm.*

Rembrandt (Harmenszoon van Rijn) (1606-69) was the greatest of the Dutch old master painters. He did many group portraits and self-portraits. Among his works are *The Night Watch* and *Syndics of the Cloth Guild.*

Rubens, Peter Paul (1577-1640), a Flemish painter, master of the baroque style. He painted portraits, landscapes, and religious and historical subjects.

Turner, Joseph M. W. (1775-1851) was a British landscape painter. He painted in both watercolors and oils. His atmospheric paintings include *The Fighting Téméraire* and *Old Chain Pier at Brighton.*

Van Gogh, Vincent (1853-90), a Dutch painter, was famous for his use of color. His paintings include *Sunflowers* and *Starry Night.*

Warhol, Andy (1926-87) was a U.S. pioneer in "pop art." He painted pop culture objects, such as Campbell's soup cans, and comic-strip characters.

Wren, Sir Christopher (1632-1723) is considered the greatest English architect. His best-known creation was St. Paul's Cathedral in London.

Wright, Frank Lloyd (1869-1959), the greatest U.S. architect of the 20th century, designed such masterpieces as the Falling Water House and the Guggenheim Museum.

WRITERS

Alcott, Louisa May (1832-88), a U.S. author, is best known for the novel *Little Women*, a story about the four March sisters and their family during the Civil War.

Andersen, Hans Christian (1805-75), a Danish writer, was one of the world's greatest storytellers. He is best known for his fairy tales, such as "The Emperor's New Clothes," "The Snow Queen," "The Little Mermaid," and "The Ugly Duckling."

Austen, Jane (1775-1817), an English novelist, wrote about the middle class of English country life in such novels as *Emma*, *Pride and Prejudice*, and *Sense and Sensibility.*

Cervantes, Miguel (1547-1616) was a Spanish novelist and dramatist. His greatest work, *Don Quixote*, details the life of a poor gentleman who wants to be a knight and do knightly deeds.

Chaucer, Geoffrey (c.1345-1400) was an English poet whose most famous work was a group of stories called the *Canterbury Tales.*

Cooper, James Fenimore (1789-1851) wrote novels about the American frontier in the 1700s. His most famous book was *The Last of the Mohicans.*

Dante Alighieri (1265-1321) was Italy's greatest poet. His most famous work was the *Divine Comedy.*

Dickens, Charles (1812-70) was one of England's greatest novelists. Some of his novels, including *Oliver Twist* and *David Copperfield*, drew attention to the plight of the poor and underprivileged.

Louisiana Purchase doubles size of U.S. 1803

War of 1812 1812–15

U.S. defeats Mexico in Mexican War; California Gold Rush begins 1848

North and South fight Civil War 1861–65

President Abraham Lincoln assassinated; 13th Amendment abolishes slavery 1865

1854 Japan opens its doors to trade with the West

1859 Darwin writes *Origin of Species*

1869 Suez Canal opens

1870 France defeated in Franco-Prussian War

1870–1914 European colonization of Africa and Asia

1894–95 China defeated in Sino-Japanese War

Dickinson, Emily (1830–86)
was one of the most important U.S. poets of the 1800s. She wrote 1,775 poems, but only a few were published when she was alive.

Frost, Robert (1874–1963)
was one of the most important U.S. poets of the 20th century. He wrote about the people and the land of New England. Among his books of poetry are *New Hampshire* and *In the Clearing*.

Goethe, Johann Wolfgang von (1749–1832)
was a poet, novelist, and playwright of unequaled importance in German literature. His greatest work was *Faust*.

Hawthorne, Nathaniel (1804–64),
born in Massachusetts, was one of the most important American writers of the 1800s. His greatest novel was *The Scarlet Letter*.

Henry, O. (1862–1910)
was one of America's foremost short-story writers. His real name was William Sydney Porter. He wrote more than 300 stories, many with surprise endings. One of his most popular stories is "The Gift of the Magi."

Keats, John (1795–1821),
an English poet, wrote beautiful odes, including "To a Nightingale," "On a Grecian Urn," and "To Autumn."

Longfellow, Henry Wadsworth (1807–82)
was a modern language professor and popular poet who wrote poems about American history including such long poems as *The Song of Hiawatha*.

Melville, Herman (1819–91)
was one of the great U.S. writers. He used his experiences as a sailor when writing his most popular books, *Moby Dick* and *Typee*.

Poe, Edgar Allan (1809–49),
a U.S. author, has been called the father of modern mystery and horror stories. His short stories include, "The Fall of the House of Usher," and "The Pit and the Pendulum." Poems include "The Raven" and "The Bells."

Sandburg, Carl (1878–1967)
was one of the most beloved U.S poets, as well as a biographer. His biography of Abraham Lincoln won the 1940 Pulitzer Prize for history.

Shakespeare, William (1564–1616),
an English dramatist and poet, is considered by many to be the world's greatest writer. His plays include *A Midsummer Night's Dream*, *Hamlet*, and *Macbeth*.

Stevenson, Robert Louis (1850–94)
was a versatile Scottish author. He wrote *A Child's Garden of Verses*, and such adventure stories as *Treasure Island* and *Kidnapped*.

Stowe, Harriet Beecher (1811–96),
a U.S. author, was famous for her novel *Uncle Tom's Cabin*. It made a powerful case against slavery.

Swift, Jonathan (1667–1745)
was an English writer whose books poked fun at the silly, cruel behavior of people and governments. His most famous book is *Gulliver's Travels*.

Tolstoy, Count Leo (1828–1910)
was a Russian novelist. Two of his greatest books were *War and Peace* and *Anna Karenina*.

Twain, Mark (1835–1910)
was a popular U.S. novelist and journalist. His real name was Samuel Clemens. Among his bestselling books were *The Adventures of Tom Sawyer* and *The Adventures of Huckleberry Finn*.

Wordsworth, William (1770–1850)
was one of England's greatest poets. His poetry explores the lives of ordinary people in contact with nature. Together with his friend Samuel Taylor Coleridge, he wrote the *Lyrical Ballads*, which included his poem "Tintern Abbey."

COMPOSERS AND MUSICIANS

Bach, Johann Sebastian (1685–1750),
a German, was one of the world's greatest composers. He wrote concertos and sacred cantatas. His masterpieces include the six *Brandenburg Concertos*, *St. Matthew Passion*, and *B Minor Mass*.

Beethoven, Ludwig van (1770–1827),
a German, wrote sonatas, symphonies, choral and chamber music, and concertos. Major works include his Ninth Symphony, the Piano Concerto no. 5, and the opera *Fidelio*.

Berlin, Irving (1888–1989)
was one of the greatest U.S. writers of popular music. He wrote nearly 1,000 songs, including "*Alexander's Ragtime Band*," "*This Is the Army*," and "*God Bless America*."

Bizet, Georges (1838–75),
a French composer, is most famous for his opera *Carmen*.

Brahms, Johannes (1833–97),
a German Romantic composer and gifted pianist, wrote piano sonatas, symphonies, and choral works.

Britten, Benjamin (1913–76),
a British composer, wrote such operas as *Billy Budd* and *Death in Venice*. He also wrote large-scale instrumental works, including *The Young Person's Guide to the Orchestra*.

Copland, Aaron (1900–90),
U.S. composer best known for using jazz and American folk tunes in his classical compositions. His works include the music for such ballets as *Billy the Kid*, *Rodeo*, and *Appalachian Spring*.

Ellington, Duke (1899–1974)
was the greatest U.S. jazz composer. He wrote more than 2,000 jazz compositions, plus concert works, religious music, and scores for theater, ballet, and film.

Gershwin, George (1898–1937)
was one of the most important U.S. songwriters of the 20th century. He produced many concert works and Broadway musicals. Gershwin's best-known works include *Porgy and Bess*, an opera, and *Rhapsody in Blue*, an orchestral work.

Handel, Georg Frideric (1685–1759),
a German-born British composer, was famous for the oratorio *Messiah*. His orchestral works include *Water Music* and *Music for the Royal Fireworks*.

Haydn, Franz Joseph (1732–1809),
an Austrian composer, was the most famous composer of his day, and he is known as the "father of the symphony." His output included 104 symphonies, about 50 concertos, and 84 string quartets, among other works.

Ives, Charles (1874–1954)
was one of the most important U.S. composers of the 20th century. His works

Tolstoy introduced a new form of Christianity into Russia, writing religious works as well as novels.

Tom Sawyer's adventures on the Mississippi River were based on Twain's own boyhood experiences.

Beethoven's music is among the greatest in the world and still influences composers today.

Duke Ellington was one of America's best-known jazz band leaders of the 1930s. He wrote over 50 hits.

1867 U.S. buys Alaska from Russia

1898 Spanish-American War; U.S. annexes Hawaii

1917–18 U.S. fights in World War I

1920 19th Amendment gives women the vote

1930s Great Depression

1941–45 U.S. fights in World War II

1904–5 Russia defeated in Russo-Japanese War

1912 Chinese overthrow Manchu Dynasty; establish republic

1914–18 World War I

1917 Communists seize power in Russia

1929 Wall Street Crash starts worldwide depression

1933 Hitler comes to power in Germany

1936–39 Civil war in Spain

Mozart began writing music at the age of five. Two years later, he was playing in concerts.

Marie and Pierre Curie devoted their lives to research, spending their own money on equipment.

Edison's first phonograph, a recording machine, led to the development of the record player.

Aristotle studied under Plato for 20 years before becoming tutor to Alexander the Great.

included symphonies, sonatas, and orchestral, choral, and chamber music. He also wrote some 150 songs. Many of his compositions used themes from American folk music.

Monteverdi, Claudio (1567-1643),
an Italian composer, wrote *Orfeo*, which is considered to be the first opera.

Mozart, Wolfgang Amadeus (1756-91),
an Austrian, was one of the world's greatest composers. He began composing at the age of five and eventually wrote more than 600 pieces of music, including symphonies, piano concertos, and operas such as *Don Giovanni* and *The Marriage of Figaro*.

Rodgers, Richard (1902-79)
was one of the most successful U.S. composers in the history of entertainment. He wrote the music for such Broadway musicals as *Oklahoma!*, *Pal Joey*, *The King and I*, *South Pacific*, and *The Sound of Music*.

Sousa, John Philip (1854-1932)
wrote so many U.S. marches he was known as the "March King." His most famous works include "The Stars and Stripes Forever," The Washington Post March," and "Semper Fidelis."

Stravinsky, Igor (1882-1971),
a Russian-born U.S. composer, wrote symphonies and operas, as well as the music for such ballets as *The Firebird* and *The Rite of Spring*.

Tchaikovsky, Peter Ilyich (1840-93)
was a Russian composer. He wrote ballet music, symphonies, piano concertos, and operas. Among his best-known works are the ballet *Swan Lake* and his First Piano Concerto.

Verdi, Giuseppe (1813-1901)
was the leading Italian operatic composer of his day. *Rigoletto*, *La Traviata*, and *Aida* are among his best-known works.

Vivaldi, Antonio (c.1675-1741)
was a Venetian violinist and composer. He wrote operas, sacred music, and concertos such as *The Four Seasons*.

Wagner, Richard (1813-83),
a German composer, is best known for his opera cycle *The Ring of the Nibelung*, which consists of four works based on old Germanic mystical legends.

SCIENTISTS AND INVENTORS

Bell, Alexander Graham (1847-1922),
a Scottish-born American, invented the telephone.

Benz, Karl (1844-19129),
a German engineer, built the first practical gasoline-powered automobile.

Copernicus, Nicolaus (1473-1543),
a Polish astronomer, proved that the Earth moves in orbit around the Sun.

Curie, Marie (1867-1934),
a Polish physicist, discovered radium, a radioactive substance. She worked with her husband Pierre.

Daguerre, Louis (1789-1851),
a French painter, invented the first practical photographic process.

Darwin, Charles (1809-82),
a British naturalist, formulated the theory of evolution by natural selection.

Edison, Thomas Alva (1847-1931),
a U.S. inventor, patented more than a thousand inventions, including the telegraph and electric lightbulb.

Einstein, Albert (1879-1955),
a German-born American physicist, changed our view of the universe with his General Theory of Relativity (1915).

Faraday, Michael (1791-1867),
a British physicist and chemist, was a pioneer in the field of electricity. His work made the dynamo and the electric motor possible.

Fermi, Enrico (1901-54),
an Italian nuclear physicist, built the first nuclear reactor.

Fleming, Alexander (1881-1955),
a British bacteriologist, discovered penicillin, the first antibiotic.

Franklin, Benjamin (1706-90),
a U.S. scientist, publisher, and statesman, proved that lightning is a form of electricity.

Galilei, Galileo (1564-1642),
an Italian astronomer and physicist, was the first to use the telescope. He also showed that light objects fall as fast as heavy ones when they are pulled toward the Earth by gravity.

Gutenberg, Johann (c.1400-68),
a German printer, was the first to develop a way to print books with speed and accuracy.

Harvey, William (1578-1657),
a British physician, discovered that the heart acted as a pump to circulate blood through the body.

Kepler, Johannes (1571-1630),
a German astronomer, showed that the planets went around the Sun in elliptical paths.

Marconi, Guglielmo (1874-1937),
an Italian-born British engineer, was the first person to transmit long-distance radio signals.

Mendel, Gregor (1822-84),
an Austrian priest, biologist, and botanist, researched the laws of heredity using pea plants.

Morse, Samuel F.B. (1791-1872),
a U.S. inventor, invented the first successful electric telegraph (1837).

Newton, Isaac (1642-1727),
an English mathematician, devised laws of motion, theorized about gravity, and showed the nature of light and color.

Pasteur, Louis (1822-95),
a French scientist, proved that disease is spread by bacteria, or germs.

Rutherford, Sir Ernest (1871-1937),
a New Zealand-born British physicist, was a pioneer in the study of the atom's structure. His work led to the development of nuclear energy.

Watt, James (1736-1819),
British engineer who improved the steam engine to make it a suitable power plant for all kinds of machinery.

Wright, Orville (1871-1948) and Wilbur (1867-1912),
two U.S. aeronautical engineers, built and flew (1903) the first successful heavier-than-air aircraft.

PHILOSOPHERS AND REFORMERS

Aristotle (384-322 B.C.),
a Greek philosopher, studied under Plato. He opened a school of philosophy in Athens. His work gave rise to the science of logical reasoning.

1950–53 Korean War

1954 School segregation ruled unconstitutional

1962 Cuban missile crisis

1963 President John F. Kennedy assassinated

1965 U.S. combat troops enter Vietnam War

1968 Martin Luther King, Jr. assassinated

1969 Neil Armstrong first to walk on the Moon

1939-45; 1945 World War II; United Nations founded  | 1949 Communists take over China | 1952 EU founded | 1957-75 Vietnam War | 1979 Islamic Revolution in Iran  | 1989-90 Democracy sweeps Eastern Europe | 1992 Yugoslavia breaks up | 1994 Black rule comes to South Africa

Calvin, John (1509-64)
was a French religious reformer and leader of the Protestant Reformation. He believed that all people, not just bishops and kings, should share in religious and political policy making.

Confucius (c. 551-c. 480 B.C.)
was a Chinese philosopher whose teachings on moral responsibility have been a strong influence on Chinese thinking for over 2,000 years.

Gandhi, Mohandas Karamchand (1869-1948),
Indian spiritual and political leader, helped free India from British control through nonviolent resistance. He was known as Mahatma, or "Great Soul."

Gautama, Siddhartha (Buddha) (c. 563-483 B.C.),
Indian religious teacher, founder of Buddhism, one of the world's great religions. He gave up his life as a prince to become a wandering monk in search of enlightenment.

Jesus Christ (c. 4 B.C.-c. A.D. 33)
was the great religious leader on whose teachings the Christian religion was founded.

Joan of Arc, Saint (c. 1412-1431),
French national leader and heroine, believed God had chosen her to free France from English rule and led French armies to many victories.

King, Martin Luther (1929-68)
was a black American minister and leader of the U.S. civil rights movement. King won the 1964 Nobel Peace Prize, but was assassinated four years later.

Luther, Martin (1483-1546)
was a German religious reformer and leader of the Reformation—the religious movement that led to the birth of Protestantism.

Marx, Karl (1818-83)
was a German political philosopher and main founder of the socialist and communist movements. Wrote *The Communist Manifesto*, with Friedrich Engels, and *Das Kapital*.

Montessori, Maria (1870-1952),
Italian educator and doctor, she designed an educational system to help children develop their intelligence and independence. This system is used throughout the world.

Mother Teresa of Calcutta (1910-1997)
was a Roman Catholic nun born in Yugoslavia. She founded a religious order in Calcutta in 1950 called Missionaries of Charity, which has branches in about 30 other countries.

Muhammad (A.D. 570-632)
was an Arabian prophet and founder of the Islamic religion. He felt himself called as God's prophet and preached that there is only one God (Allah).

Nightingale, Florence (1820-1910),
English nursing pioneer, reformed the nursing profession.

Pankhurst, Emmeline (1858-1928)
was an English political reformer. She led the fight for women's right to vote in England.

Plato (c. 427-c.347BC),
a Greek philosopher, founded what is probably the first-ever university, known as the Academy. He wrote *The Republic*, in which he outlined the ideal state or society.

Sanger, Margaret (1883-1966)
was the American leader of the birth control movement.

Socrates (c. 469-399 B.C.),
a Greek philosopher and teacher, devoted himself to seeking truth and goodness.

Stanton, Elizabeth Cady (1815-1902)
was a leader of the U.S. women's rights movement. She also worked for the abolition of slavery.

Wesley, John (1703-91),
English clergyman, founder of Methodism. He traveled over 5,000 miles a year, preaching.

Wilberforce, William (1759-1833)
was an English politician and reformer. He led the fight to abolish slavery in the British Empire.

Wollstonecraft, Mary (1759-97)
was an English author who argued that women should have equal rights to men in her book, *A Vindication of the Rights of Women.*

EXPLORERS

Amundsen, Roald (1872-1928),
a Norwegian, discovered the Northwest Passage and was the first man to reach the South Pole (1911).

Balboa, Vasco Núñez de (1475-1519),
a Spaniard, was the first European to sight the east coast of the Pacific Ocean (1513).

Bird, Richard E. (1888-1957),
a U.S. polar explorer, was the first to fly over the North Pole (1926) and the South Pole (1929).

Cabot, John (c.1461-98),
an Italian-born English explorer, claimed North American territory for England.

Champlain, Samuel de (1567-1635),
a French explorer, explored the Atlantic coast of Canada and founded Quebec (1608).

Columbus, Christopher (1451-1506),
an Italian explorer, discovered the New World while seeking a route to Asia.

Cook, James (1728-79),
an English sea captain, was the first to sight Antarctica and explore the Pacific Ocean.

Cortés, Hernán (1485-1547),
a Spanish explorer, conquered the Aztec Empire of Mexico (1521).

Da Gama, Vasco (c.1469-1524),
Portuguese navigator and explorer, sailed around Africa to India and back to Europe.

Ericsson, Leif (fl. 900-1000),
a Viking sailor, was the first European to land in North America (c.1000).

Livingstone, David (1813-73),
a Scottish explorer, traveled through much of Africa's interior.

Magellan, Ferdinand (c.1480-1521),
a Portuguese explorer, led the first expedition to sail around the world (1519-22). He was killed by natives in the Philippines before the journey was completed.

Peary, Robert E. (1856-1920),
a U.S. explorer, claimed to be the first person to reach the North Pole (1909).

Pizarro, Francisco (c.1475-1541),
a Spanish explorer, conquered the Inca Empire of Peru (1533).

Polo, Marco (c.1254-1324),
a Venetian (Italian) explorer, traveled through Asia and met Kublai Khan, the Mongol emperor.

Elizabeth Cady Stanton began the U.S. women's suffrage movement in 1848.

Gandhi is often called the "father of modern India" for his work in freeing India from British rule.

Vasco da Gama reached India in 1498 by sailing around the Cape of Good Hope in southern Africa.

Henry Morton Stanley, a reporter, found Livingstone (feared dead in Africa) at Lake Tanganyika in 1871.

Vietnam War ends 1975 | U.S. invades Panama 1989 | U.S. and Allies defeat Iraq in Persian Gulf War 1991 | Truck bomb kills 168 in Oklahoma City 1995 | U.S. peacekeeping troops arrive in Bosnia 1995 | Timothy McVeigh sentenced to death for Oklahoma City bombing 1997

HIGHLIGHTS OF THE 20TH CENTURY

In Germany, Adolf Hitler's aggressive policies led to the outbreak of WW II.

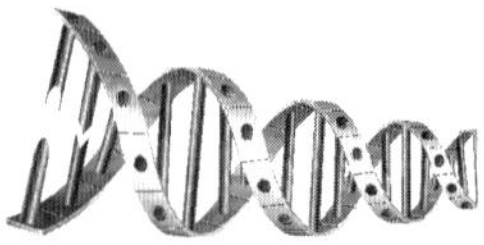

DNA determines which traits children inherit from their parents.

Personal computers became commonly available in the early 1980s.

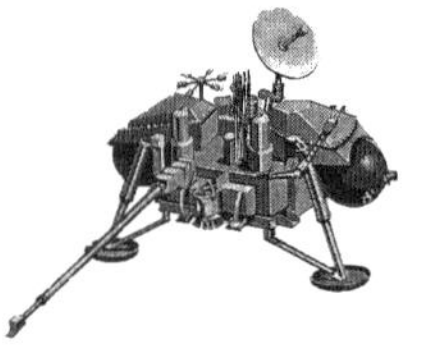

U.S. spacecraft *Viking I* and *2* landed probes on Mars by parachute.

Half of the world's robots, such as this automated arm, are used in Japan.

In 1953, Hillary and Tenzing were the first to scale Mt. Everest.

SPACE EXPLORATION

1957: The Soviet Union launches *Sputnik 1*, the first artificial satellite to orbit the Earth.
1961: Soviet cosmonaut Yuri Gagarin, aboard the *Vostok 1* spacecraft, becomes the first man to orbit the Earth.
1962: Astronaut John H. Glenn, Jr., aboard the *Mercury 6* spacecraft, becomes the first American to orbit the Earth.
1963: Soviet cosmonaut Valentina Tereshkova orbits the Earth in the *Vostok 6* spacecraft, becoming the first woman in space.
1965: Soviet cosmonaut Aleksei Leonov takes the first space walk.
1968: *Apollo 8* becomes the first spacecraft to orbit the Moon.
1969: *Apollo 11* astronauts Neil Armstrong and Edwin Aldrin become the first men to land on the Moon.
1970: *Venera 7*, a Soviet spacecraft, lands on Venus and transmits data back to Earth.
1975: The Soviet Union's *Venera 7* takes the first photographs of the surface of Venus.
1976: *Viking 1* and *Viking 2*, U.S. spacecraft, land on Mars and send photos and data back to Earth.
1977: The United States launches *Voyager 2*, which will later photograph Jupiter (1979), Saturn (1981), Uranus (1986), and Neptune (1989).
1981: The United States launches the space shuttle *Columbia*, the first reusable manned spacecraft.
1986: The U.S. space shuttle *Challenger* blows up shortly after launch, killing all seven astronauts.
1990: The U.S. space probe *Magellan* orbits Venus and sends radar images of the planet back to Earth. The Hubble Space Telescope is launched.
1997: The U.S. Mars *Pathfinder* spacecraft lands on Mars and deploys *Sojourner*, a roving vehicle to analyze Martian rocks and soil.
1998: Water is discovered frozen in rocks on the Moon.

POLITICAL EVENTS

1914: World War I starts when Archduke Francis Ferdinand of Austria is assassinated. The war ends in 1918.
1917: The Communists seize power in Russia during the Russian Revolution.
1929: The Wall Street Crash sets off the Great Depression.
1933: Adolf Hitler becomes the dictator of Germany.
1939: The German invasion of Poland starts World War II.
1941: The United States enters World War II after Japan attacks Pearl Harbor.
1945: World War II ends after the United States drops two atomic bombs on Japan. Tens of millions of people were killed during the war, including six million Jews killed in the Holocaust. The United Nations is founded.
1948: The state of Israel is founded.
1949: The Communists take control of China.
1950: Communist North Korea invades South Korea, starting the Korean War. The fighting ended three years later.
1952: European Community (now European Union), is founded.
1965: U.S. combat troops enter the Vietnam War. The war ends with the defeat of the U.S. in 1973.
1989: Communism begins to collapse in Eastern Europe, with democratic governments replacing communist dictatorships.
1990: Apartheid ends and black rule begins in South Africa.
1991: The Soviet Union ceases to exist and breaks up into 15 independent states.

SCIENCE AND MEDICINE

1905: German-born U.S. physicist Albert Einstein publishes his special theory of relativity.
1913: Hungarian-born pediatrician Bela Schick discovers an immunity test for diphtheria.
1915: Physicist Albert Einstein publishes his general theory of relativity.
1921: Canadian physicians Frederick Banting and Charles Best discover the hormone insulin, a treatment for diabetes.
1928: Scottish bacteriologist Alexander Fleming discovers penicillin, the first antibiotic.
1942: U.S. physicist Enrico Fermi directs the first controlled nuclear reaction.
1945: The first atomic bomb is detonated in New Mexico.
1953: Biologists Francis Crick (U.K.) and James Watson (U.S.) discover the structure of deoxyribonucleic acid (DNA), the actual material that chromosomes are made of.
1954: Harvard University physicians perform the first successful organ (kidney) transplant.
1955: U.S. microbiologist Jonas Salk develops the first vaccine against polio, a crippling disease.
1967: South African surgeon Christiaan Barnard performs the first heart transplant.
1982: U.S. surgeons working at the Utah Medical Center implant the first artificial heart.
1997: Scottish scientists are the first to clone a sheep.

TELECOMMUNICATIONS

1901: Italian-born inventor Guglielmo Marconi, using Morse code-like dot-and-dash signals, sends the first radio message across the Atlantic Ocean.
1915: First transcontinental telephone call between inventor Alexander Graham Bell in New York and his assistant Thomas Watson in San Francisco, over 3,000 miles away.
1906: U.S. engineer Reginald A. Fessendon broadcasts the first radio program of voice and music.
1929: Russian-born American electronic engineer Vladimir Zworykin demonstrates the first electronic television system.
1936: The British Broadcasting Corporation makes the first television broadcasts.
1946: U.S. engineers J. Presper Eckert, Jr. and John W. Mauchly build ENIAC, the first electronic digital computer.
1947: Bell Telephone Laboratories develops the first transistor.
1951: Eckert and Mauchly build UNIVAC I, the first commercially available computer.
1953: Color television broadcast begins in the United States.
Early 1960s: The integrated circuit is developed.
1961: Bell Telephone Laboratories builds the first practical laser.
1965: Early Bird, the first commercial communications satellite, is launched.
1977: The Apple Computer Company introduces the first personal computer.
1983: Cellular phone service begins.

INDEX

Bold numbers before colons refer to volume numbers. Page numbers in bold type refer to key topics. Page numbers in italic type refer to illustrations and maps.

A

B

ACKNOWLEDGMENTS

The publishers wish to thank the following for supplying photographs for this book:

ABBREVIATIONS
(*t* = top; *b* = bottom; *c* = center; *l* = left; *r* = right)

PICTURE LIBRARY ABBREVIATIONS
AAA: The Ancient Art & Architecture Collection; **AKG:** AKG UK Ltd; **BAL:** The Bridgeman Art Library; **B&C Alexander:** Bryan & Cherry Alexander; **BC:** Bruce Coleman Collection; **EB/JD:** Eye Ubiquitous/James Davis Travel Agency; **ET:** E.T. Archive; **FLPA:** Frank Lane Picture Agency; **FS:** Frank Spooner Pictures; **GI:** Getty Images; **HL:** The Hutchison Library; **NHPA:** Natural History Photographic Agency; **OSF:** Oxford Scientific Films; **Panos:** Panos Pictures; **PE:** Planet Earth Pictures; **Popper:** Popperfoto; **RGA:** The Ronald Grant Archive; **RHPL:** Robert Harding Picture Library; **SP:** Still Pictures; **SPL:** Science Photo Library

Pages: **viii:** Colorific **1: 1** NHPA, GI *(tr)* **1: 2** RHPL *(tr)*, NHPA *(b)* **1: 3** Still Pictures *(b)* **1: 4** SP *(tl)*, RHPL *(bl)*, Panos *(br)* **1: 4/5** RHPL *(tc)* **1: 5** The British Museum *(b)*, AllSport UK *(tr)* **1: 8** Telegraph Colour Library *(tr)* **1: 9** OSF *(tr)* **1: 10** PE *(tr)* **1: 12** NHPA *(tl)*, PE *(tr)* **1: 16** Popper *(tl)*, BC *(cr)*, NHPA *(bl)* **1: 17** The British Museum *(bl)*, AAA *(br)* **1: 19** RHPL *(b)* **1: 20** NHPA *(cr)*, B&C Alexander *(bc)* **1: 21** RHPL *(cl)*, GI *(cr)*, HL *(br)* **1: 22** AKG *(tr, c)*, BAL *(tl, cl, cr, bl, br)* **1: 23** AKG *(tl, cr)*, ET *(tr)*, ©Duane Hanson/Saatchi Collection *(bl)*, BAL *(br)* **1: 24** SP *(tr)*, NHPA *(bl)*, RHPL *(b)* **1: 25** Panos *(b)* **1: 26** HL *(tl/b)*, FS *(tr)* **1: 27** Panos *(tr, bl)*, BAL *(bc)* **1: 28** Portfolio Pictures *(bl)*, SPL *(tr)*, Space Photo Library *(bc)*, NASA *(br)* **1: 32** SPL *(tl, tr)* **1: 34** PE *(tr)*, OSF *(bc)* **1: 35** PE *(bc)*, NHPA *(br)* **1: 36** Colorific *(tl)*, SP *(bc)* **1: 37** RHPL *(tl)*, Colorific *(tr)*, NHPA *(c)* **1: 40** Virgin *(cl)*, Images Colour Library *(tr)* **1: 43** GI *(tr)* **1: 44** SPL *(tr)***1: 47** NHPA *(cr)* **2: 1** SPL *(br)* **2: 2** Corbis *(tl)*, SPL *(tr)* **2: 3** Zefa *(br)* **2: 6** EB/JD *(tr)*, RHPL *(cl)*, GI *(b)* **2: 7** GI *(cl)*, EB/JD *(br)* **2: 9** Graham Harrison *(tr)*, GI *(cl, br)* **2: 10** OSF *(cl)* **2: 11** BC *(ct, cb)* **2: 12** Zefa *(tr)*, RHPL *(cl/b)*, Robert Estall Photo Library *(cr)* **2: 13** BC *(cl)*, RHPL *(br)* **2: 14** Panos *(tr)*, HL *(b)* **2: 15** HL *(cl)*, SuperStock *(br)* **2: 16** AllSport UK *(tr)* **2: 17** Ford Motor Company *(tr)* **2: 18** RGA *(tl, ct, cb)*, Portfolio Pictures *(tr)*, SP *(br)* **2: 22** SPL *(l)* **2: 23** The National Museum of Ireland *(tl)*, AAA *(c)*, BAL *(bl)* **2: 24** RHPL *(tr)*, Panos *(b)* **2: 25** GI *(tr, b)*, Panos *(cl)* **2: 27** BC *(tr)*, SP *(cl)*, Image Bank *(b)* **2: 28** BC *(b)* **2: 29** RHPL *(tc)*, GI *(tr, bl)*, RHPL *(br)* **2: 30** Panos *(tr, bl, br)* **2: 31** GI *(c, bcl)*, Zefa *(bl)*, FS *(bcr)*, Rex Features *(br)* **2: 32** Amnesty International *(tl)*, Popper *(tr)*, Corbis *(b)* **2: 33** Corbis *(tl)*, AFP *(bl)*, Camera Press *(br)* **2: 34** Peter Newark Library *(tl)* **2: 38** RHPL *(tr)*, Camera Press *(cl)* **2: 39** Zefa *(tc)*, FS *(tr)*, GI *(c)*, RHPL *(br)* **2: 40** RHPL *(c)* **2: 41** Corbis *(b)* **2: 42** AKG *(tr)* **2: 43** SPL *(tl, bl)* **2: 44** GI *(tr)* **2: 45** Camera Press *(cl, bl)*, AKG *(br)* **2: 47** Corbis *(tr)* GI *(cr)* **2: 48** SPL *(tl)*, AKG *(tr)* **3: 2** Travel Ink *(tr)* **3: 8** RHPL *(br)* **3: 10** Allsport UK/Vandystadt *(bl)*, Performing Arts Library *(br)* **3: 11** EB/JD *(tl)*, Rex Features *(tr)*, Performing Arts Library *(c, br)* **3: 12** Popper *(b)* **3: 13** GI *(tl)* **3: 14** RHPL *(tl)* **3: 18** FS *(tl)*, SPL *(bl)* **3: 19** Farmers Weekly *(br)* **3: 24** Rex Features *(b)* **3: 25** Panos *(tr)*, GI *(b)* **3: 26** Panos *(b)* **3: 27** Panos *(tl)*, GI *(tr)*, Rex Features *(b)* **3: 28** Panos *(br)* **3: 29** Panos *(tl)*, EB/JD *(cl)*, GI *(cr, b)* **3: 30** GI *(l, b)* **3: 31** Simon Farrell *(tr)* **3: 37** GI *(cr)* **3: 38** RHPL *(tr)* **3: 40** Popper *(tl)*, Colorsport *(tr)*, UPI *(cl)* **3: 42** FLPA *(tr)*, GI *(b)* **3: 43** FLPA *(br)* **3: 44** Zefa *(tl)*, GI *(tr)*, Rex Features *(bl)* **3: 45** GI *(tr)*, RHPL *(cl)*, Rex Features *(b)* **4: 1** W.J. Hatt Ltd, The Institute of Explosive *(tl, tc, bl, bc, br)* **4: 2** Topham *(cl)* **4: 3** Popper *(tl, ct, bl)*, Camera Press *(cb)*, Corbis *(bl)* **4: 6** NHPA *(tr)* **4: 8** FLPA *(cr)* **4: 13** NHPA *(tr)* **4: 14** RHPL *(bl)*, **4: 14/15** GI *(c)* **4: 15** GI *(c)* **4: 16** Telegraph Colour Library *(tr)* **4: 17** Robin Keeley *(tl)*, Topham *(cl)* **4: 18** GI *(tl)* **4: 20** GI *(tr, cl, b)* **4: 21** FS *(tl)*, Popper *(cl)*, RHPL *(cr)* **4: 24** SPL *(tr)* **4: 25** SPL *(tl)* **4: 26** SP *(bl)*, Telegraph Colour Library *(bcl, br)*, GI *(bcr)* **4: 27** Popper *(tr)* **4: 28** Zefa *(tr)*, FS *(cl)*, RHPL *(b)* **4: 29** Popper *(cl)*, GI *(b)* **4: 32** Sonia Halliday Photographs *(cl)* **4: 33** SPL *(tr, bc)*, The Wallace Collection, London *(cl)* **4: 34** RHPL *(cr)*, Topham *(bl)* **4: 35** NHPA *(tl)* **4: 36** Corbis *(cl)*, GI *(b)* **4: 37** Corbis *(tr, cr)* **4: 38** GI *(tr, b)* **4: 39** Popper *(tl)*, RHPL *(cl)*, Panos *(br)* **4: 41** RHPL *(tr)* **4: 42** NHPA *(tr, cl)*, PE *(tl, bcl, bcr)*, GI *(cr)* **4: 45** RHPL *(tr)* **4: 48** FS *(tr)*, GI *(b)* **5: 1** BC *(tr)* **5: 2** Image Bank *(b)* **5: 3** GI *(br)* **5: 4** Transcolour *(tr)* **5: 5** GI *(tr)*, Panos *(bl)*, Zefa *(br)* **5: 6** OSF *(tr)* **5: 7** EB/JD *(t, c, bc)*, Panos *(tc, b)* **5: 8** GI *(tl)*, FS *(cl)* **5: 9** Image Bank *(tc)* **5: 12** Panos *(tr)*, GI *(b)* **5: 13** Panos *(c)* Image Bank *(bl)* **5: 14** Colorific Photo Library *(tl)*, GI *(tr)*, FS *(b)* **5: 15** OSF *(tl)*, Corbis *(tr)*, Panos *(bl)* **5: 16** GI *(cl, bl)*, Panos *(cr)* **5: 18** GI *(tl)* **5: 20** RHPL *(tr)*, Panos *(cr)* **5: 21** OSF *(cr, br)* **5: 22** OSF, BC *(br)* **5: 24** FS *(tr)* **5: 25** BAL *(tr)* **5: 26** GI *(cl, bl)*, The Houghton's Horses *(br)* **5: 27** GI *(tr)* **5: 28** RHPL *(cl)*, GI *(b)* **5: 29** FLPA *(tr)*, GI *(cl)*, Network Photography/Mike Abraham *(bl)* **5: 30** GI *(b)* **5: 31** FS *(cr)*, John Ferro Sims *(bl)* **5: 32** GI *(tr, b)*, Panos *(cl)* **5: 33** RHPA *(cr)*, Zefa *(b)* **5: 34** Zefa *(tr)* **5: 35** GI *(tr, cl)*, Image Bank *(bl)*, Colorific Photo Library *(cb)* **5: 37** Panos *(cl)*, PE *(bl)*, GI *(br)* **5: 38** SPL *(tl)* **5: 40** EB/JD *(tl)*, BAL *(b)* **5: 41** RHPL *(tl)*, Zefa *(tr, bl)*, The Research House *(cl)* **5: 42** Image Bank *(tl)* **5: 45** Zefa *(tr, cr)*, Corbis *(tl)*, Image Bank *(cl)*, OSF *(bl, bc)* **5: 46** Image Bank *(tl)* **6: 4** SPL *(tr)* **6: 5** HL *(cl)*, Panos *(bl)*, RHPL *(br)* **6: 9** Image Bank *(tr)* **6: 10** Panos *(tr)* **6: 11** Alpha *(c)*, A.C. Edwards *(bl)* **6: 12** Glaxo Group Research *(tr)* **6: 13** SPL *(tr, b)* **6: 15** AAA *(cr, br)* **6: 16** Telegraph Colour Library *(tl)* **6: 17** South American Pictures *(tr)*, Spectrum Colour Library *(cl)*, Panos *(bl)* **6: 18** SPL *(l)* **6: 19** SPL *(l)*, Leo Electron Microscope *(tr)*, Leica UK *(bc)* **6: 21** RHPL *(tr)*, Panos *(b)* **6: 22** HL *(c)* **6: 23** Spectrum Colour Library *(tl)*, FS *(tr)*, HL *(bc)* **6: 24** PE *(bl)* **6: 25** OSF *(tr)* **6: 26** SP *(tl)* **6: 31** OSF *(br)* **6: 36** Zefa *(t)*, Redferns *(cl, bl, br)* **6: 37** RHPL *(b)* **6: 38** Edinburgh University *(cr)*, Keith Saunders Photography *(bc)* **6: 43** Corbis *(tr)* **6: 45** FS *(bl)* **6: 47** Spectrum Colour Library *(tc, c)*, FS *(bl)* **6: 48** Panos *(cl, b)* **7: 1** Panos *(tr)*, HL *(bl)* **7: 2** NHPA *(bl)* **7: 3** Panos *(tl)*, HL *(tr)*, Zefa *(bl)* **7: 4** Popper *(tr)* **7: 5** SP *(tr)* **7: 8** SPL *(tr)* **7: 9** AllSport *(cr)* Topham *(b)* **7: 10** Topham *(tl)* **7: 11** AllSport UK *(tr, cr)* **7: 13** SPL *(tl)* **7: 15** HL *(tr)*, Panos *(cl, c)* **7: 16** Polaroid *(cl)*, Ixus *(bl)*, BAL *(b)* **7: 17** Science & Society Picture Library *(tr)*, Nikon UK *(br)* **7: 18** HL *(tr)* **7: 21** The Kobal Collection *(bl)* **7: 24** ICI *(b)* **7: 25** NHPA *(tl, tr)* **7: 26** Corbis (t) **7: 27** HL *(b)* **7: 29** AAA *(cl)* **7: 31** Popper *(cr)* **7: 35** NHPA *(cl)* **7: 36** PE *(tr)* **7: 38** SP *(tl)*, Jean-Loup Charmet *(tr)*, Popper *(bl)* **7: 39** HL *(b)* **7: 40** BAL *(cr, bl)* **7: 42** GI *(cr)* **7: 48** Rex Features *(tl)*, Popper *(tr)*, GI *(cl)* **8: 1** PE *(tr)* **8: 2** NHPA *(bl)*, HL *(br)* **8: 4** GI *(tl)*, HL *(bc)* **8: 5** SPL *(tl, cl)*, The Kobal Collection *(tc)*, Honda Motor Company *(tr)* **8: 6:** NHPA *(tr)* **8: 7** NASA *(tr)* **8: 9** Zefa *(tr)*, GI *(cr)* **8: 10** Novosti London *(tr)*, RHPL *(b)* **8: 11** HL *(br)* **8: 12** Rex Features *(tl)*, Novosti London *(cl)*, HL *(bl, br)* **8: 14** GI *(tr, b)* **8: 15** RHPL *(bl)*, FLPA *(br)* **8: 16** AKG *(tl)*, Rex Features *(tr)*, ©Andy Goldworthy *(cl)*, GI *(b)* **8: 17** GI *(tl, cl)*, HL *(br)* **8: 18** HL *(cr)*, Spectrum Colour Library *(br)* **8: 22** Zefa *(tr)* **8: 25** RHPL *(tr)*, AAA *(c)*, Christie's Images *(cr)* **8: 26** GI *(tr, b)* **8: 29** Travel Ink *(tl)* **8: 30** BAL *(tr)*, Mary Evans Picture Library *(br)* **8: 31** SPL *(tl)*, AKG *(b)* **8: 32** OSF *(tc)* **8: 33** NHPA *(tr)* **8: 34** Zefa *(b)* **8: 35** Topham *(tr)* **8: 39** Popper *(b)* **8: 40** RHPL *(cl, tr)*, GI *(b)* **8: 41** FS *(bl)*, RHPL *(cr)* **8: 42** South American Library *(tr, cl, b)* **8: 43** HL *(tl)*, South American Library *(bl)*, Panos *(br)* **8: 44** Panos *(tl, b)*, South American Library *(tr)* **8: 45** South American Library *(tr, c)*, HL *(b)* **8: 46** Panos *(bl)* **8: 47** Panos *(tl, c)*, HL *(tr)* **9: 1** SPL *(tr)* **9: 2** SPL *(l)* **9: 4** GI *(tr)*, HL *(cl)*, RHPL *(b)* **9: 5** HL *(b)* **9: 7** NHPA *(tl)* **9: 9** Sporting Pictures *(tr)*, AllSport UK *(br)* **9: 10** Sporting Pictures *(tc)* **9: 13** NHPA *(tr)* **9: 14** SPL *(tl)*, GI *(tr)* **9: 16** HL *(cl)*, Panos *(bl)* **9: 18** AKG *(tr)*, RHPL *(b)* **9: 20** RHPL **9: 22** SPL *(b)* **9: 23** Zefa *(tr)* **9: 24** Mary Evans Picture Library *(tl)*, British Telecom *(cl)*, GI *(bl)* **9: 25** Corbis *(tr, br)*, Philips UK *(cl)* **9: 27** Simmons Ltd *(tc)*, SPL *(br)* **9: 29** AKG *(tr)*, SPL *(bl)*, RHPL *(br)* **9: 34** Topham *(tr)* **9: 35** Panos *(cl)*, RGA *(cr)*, RHPL *(b)* **9: 36** GI *(tr)* **9: 37** Panos *(b)* **9: 40** SPL *(cl)* **9: 41** FS *(br)* **9: 43** Telegraph Colour Library *(tr)* **9: 44** Greyhound Ltd *(tr)* **9: 45** GI *(bl)* **9: 46** Popper *(cl)*, RHPL *(tr)*, British Tourist Authority *(b)* **9: 47** British Tourist Authority *(tl)*, HL *(bl)*, RHPL *(br)* **9: 48** FS *(cr)*, Popper *(b)* **10: 1** Panos *(tr)*, RHPL *(bl, br)* **10: 2** RHPL *(tl, cl)*, Zefa *(br)* **10: 3** RHPL *(cl, br)* **10: 4** RHPL *(tl, cl)*, Corbis *(cr)*, Redfern *(b)* **10: 5** SPL *(tl)* **10: 6** Popper *(b)* **10: 7** Sanyo UK *(tl)*, SPL *(tr, cl)*, Sony *(br)* **10: 10** HL *(tl)* **10: 14** Topham *(br)* **10: 15** HL *(tc)* **10: 16** Corbis *(tl)* **10: 17** SPL *(tr)* **10: 19** SPL *(tc)* **10: 21** SPL *(tl)* **10: 25** RHPL *(tr)*, SPL *(b)* **10: 27** NHPA *(tc)* **10: 28** Corbis *(tr)*, Corbis *(b)* **10: 29** GI *(tl)*, Corbis *(tr)*, Popper *(bl)*, Corbis *(cr)* **10: 33** Corbis *(bl)* **10: 34** PE *(br)* **10: 35** SPL *(tr, bl)* **10: 36:** Marwell Zoo *(br)*

Illustrators

Julian Baker Illustration, Julian Baum, Michelle Brand, Andy Burton, Tom Connell, Maggie Downer, Richard Draper, Andrew Farmer, Chris Forsey, Mick Gillah, Trevor Hill, Karen Hiscock, Christian Hook, Kevin Jones Associates, Ruth Lindsay, Ceri Llewellyn, Kevin Maddison, Nicki Palin, Peter Ross, Peter Sarson, Mike Saunders, Ron Tiner, Martin Woodward, *Black Hat*: Kevin Lyles, *Blue Chip*: Keith Harmer, *David Lewis Agency*: Mark Stacey, *J.M. & A*: Steinar Lund, *Linda Rogers Associates*: Peter Dennis, *Linden Artists*: Lindsay Graham, Richard Hook, Sebastian Quigley, Clive Spong, *Specs Art*: Richard Berridge, *Virgil Pomfret*: Luigi Galanti, *W.L.A*: Cy Baker, Derick Bown, Robin Budden, Robin Carter, Barry Croucher, Sandra Doyle, Brin Edwards, David Hardy, Dan Harvey, Philip Hood, Ian Jackson, Bridgette Jones, Rachel Lockwood, Pond/Giles, Jonathan Potter, Steve Roberts, Andrew Robinson, Mike Rowe, Chris Shields, Paul Staveley, Mark Stewart, Mike Taylor, Richard Tibbitts, Chris Turnbull, Simon Turvey, David Woods

The publishers would also like to thank the following for their help in supplying information used as visual reference:

Pages: **1: 6-7** Boeing Aircraft Corporation (Boeing 747); **1: 11** Zoological Society of London (fire salamander cutaway); **1: 17** Geoscan Research (scanner); **1: 19** Ove Arup & Partners (Sydney Opera House); **1: 30-31** W.M. Keck Observatory (Keck observatory); **2: 14-15** John Willoughby, The Mustang Owners Club of Great Britain, Selby (Mustang); **4: 2** Fullwood Ltd (milking shed); **4: 46** Bell Helicopter Textron (helicopter cutaway); **5: 4** Dyson Appliances Ltd (Dyson vacuum cleaner cutaway); **5: 6** The Hovercraft Museum Trust; **6: 2-3** Otis plc, Ove Arup & Partners (elevator); **6: 12-13** Picker International Ltd, Siemens Medical Engineering (CAT scanner); **7: 4** Nuclear Electric (nuclear reactor); **7: 8** British Petroleum (platform); **7: 9-11** Olympic Museum; **8: 25** Balco Ltd (electroplating system); **9: 26** British Telecom (wall telephone); **9: 41** Ford Motor Company (people carrier)